THE
PLANTPURE
NATION
COOKBOOK

The Official Companion Cookbook
to the Breakthrough Film . . .
with over 150 Plant-Based Recipes

Kim Campbell

Foreword by T. Colin Campbell, PhD

Photographs by Brian Olson

BENBELLA

BenBella Books, Inc.
Dallas, Texas

BenBella Books, Inc.
10300 N. Central Expressway
Suite #530
Dallas, TX 75231
www.benbellabooks.com
Send feedback to feedback@benbellabooks.com
Printed in the United States of America

10 9 8 7 6 5 4 3 2

Library of Congress Cataloging-in-Publication Data
Campbell, Kim (Nutritionist)
   The PlantPure Nation cookbook : the official companion cookbook to the breakthrough film . . . with over 150 plant-based recipes / Kim Campbell ; foreword by T. Colin Campbell.
     pages   cm
   Includes index.
   ISBN 978-1-940363-68-4 (paperback)
   ISBN 978-1-940363-69-1 (electronic)
   1. Vegetarian cooking.   I. Title.
   TX837.C3268   2015
   641.5'636—dc23   2014026410

Editing by Leah Wilson and Vy Tran
Copyediting by Karen Levy
Proofreading by Kristin Vorce and Laura Cherkas
Indexing by WordCo Indexing Services
Food photography and cover photos by Brian Olson
Photographs on pages 122, 149, 174, 244, and 262 contributed by Frank Smith
Movie stills from *PlantPure Nation* courtesy of Nelson Campbell
Front cover design by Bradford Foltz
Full cover design by Sarah Dombrowsky
Text design and composition by Ralph Fowler / rlfdesign
Printed by Versa Press

Distributed by Perseus Distribution
www.perseusdistribution.com

To place orders through Perseus Distribution:
Tel: (800) 343-4499
Fax: (800) 351-5073
E-mail: orderentry@perseusbooks.com

Significant discounts for bulk sales are available.
Please contact Glenn Yeffeth at glenn@benbellabooks.com or (214) 750-3628.

To Nelson and our children,
Whitney, Colin, and Laura

CONTENTS

Page 37

Page 200

Page 255

Page 265

Spices and Toppings   145

The Mebane Experiment   149

Sandwiches, Burgers, and Wraps   151

Page 152

Page 205

PlantPure Nation Profile:
Patty Jones   174

Page 277

Entrées 175

Side Dishes 245

The Problem of Food Deserts 262

Soups and Stews 263

Taking Back Agriculture from Agribusiness 282

Desserts and Sweets 283

Page 206

Page 284

Page 295

Page 292

APPENDIX

In the following pages, Kim Campbell, my wonderful daughter-in-law of twenty-seven years, has shared the kind of recipes that I believe are essential to anyone interested in leading a plant-based lifestyle. I've sat at Kim's table for many an evening, eating the very dishes that are in this book. Kim has cooked this way for more than twenty-five years, and she has perfected the art of plant-based culinary cuisine as well as anyone I know.

These recipes have several characteristics. First, they are *tasty*. Second, they are *affordable*. Third, a substantial number of them have been used in wellness programs organized by my son Nelson and Kim, and have been proven to be *efficacious*. Fourth, they are *quick and easy to prepare*.

After being in the fields of nutrition, biochemistry, and toxicology for so long, after publishing our results in the very best scientific journals, and after being a member of several expert panels to develop national and international food and health information, I have seen much of what is troubling about our health system and what might be done to make it right.

I am convinced that the solution begins with food that is tasty, affordable, efficacious, and easy to prepare.

Not only will dining on these recipes create, maintain, and restore personal health, but doing so also benefits our society in so many ways. Controlling health care costs, minimizing environmental degradation, and restoring a sense of stewardship and peace for all sentient beings on our planet come to mind. And on that point, I also encourage you to go, if you have not already, to see the film produced by Kim's husband, Nelson, and his team, including a producer and writer who were key to the production of the highly successful film *Forks Over Knives* (which I also encourage you to watch).

Take this book, put it in a place in your kitchen that catches your eye often, and try these recipes. I am confident that you will love Kim's cooking.

—T. Colin Campbell, PhD
Professor Emeritus of Nutritional Biochemistry, Cornell University, Coauthor of the best-selling book *The China Study*

Introduction

I was sixteen years old, in a high school near Cornell and dreaming of studying nutrition, when I met my husband, Nelson Campbell, and his family.

I grew up in a small rural town. My parents were raised on dairy farms and I too lived on a family dairy farm in the beautiful Finger Lakes region of upstate New York, until my father took a job with Cornell Cooperative Extension as a dairy consultant and educator.

At that time, Nelson's father, Dr. T. Colin Campbell, was also at Cornell and in the middle of the research in China that would become the best-selling book *The China Study*. Though Colin often traveled back and forth as he gathered data and compiled results, the first time Nelson brought me home for dinner, he happened to be there.

Colin loves to talk about his research, and I love asking questions. During one of my first visits to their home, Colin spent hours showing me slides of family pictures and his travels around the world doing research. He shared what researchers were learning about the incredible differences in health between those who ate a plant-based diet and those who ate a meat- and dairy-heavy Western diet, discussing his earlier work in the Philippines and at Virginia Tech on the negative effects of animal proteins. This may not

have been what Nelson had in mind when he'd invited me—but I was fascinated.

In my teen years, I loved to cook for my parents and siblings. I'd grown up eating a traditional diet of meat and dairy, supplemented by fresh vegetables grown in my father's large gardens, but especially after meeting Nelson's family, I began experimenting with vegetarian and vegan recipes.

I went on to study nutrition at Cornell, but in my classes I met the harsh reality of nutritional instruction during that time. It was the 1980s, and plant-based nutrition was far from mainstream. Despite the incredible findings in China, Colin's colleagues, even those in his own department, were shunning, sometimes even mocking him. I became disillusioned by the ignorance, ego, and cowardice in this field. Though I still earned a minor in nutrition education, I decided on a different career path: childhood education.

As a public school teacher, I brought my passion for helping young people make the right food choices into the classroom. I incorporated food and nutrition into my curriculum any way I could, teaching my students to take responsibility for their diet and health. At home, Nelson and I did the same for our three children, and our family has been cooking and eating primarily plant-based cuisine for more than twenty-five years. But we both felt it was important to spread this knowledge further.

Over the past four years, Nelson has pursued a dream of building a socially conscious company committed to bringing his father's message into the mainstream. This company has developed a foods-based wellness program that brings the benefits of plant-based eating to a larger, more diverse audience. I've been fortunate to play my own part in this effort, providing culinary education and consultation for our clients, and helping in the development and testing of the meals used in the program. It's a role that allows me to apply all the knowledge I've gained over the past twenty-five years, and seeing the differences the program has made in our clients' lives has been nothing short of exhilarating.

PlantPure Nation, spearheaded by Nelson, grew directly out of our work in wellness. The film shows the impact plant-based nutrition has had on the health and well-being of the rural North Carolina community of Mebane. It also addresses the larger political issues surrounding the idea of plant-based nutrition, especially why this idea has been suppressed for so long.

The core of the wellness program shown in the film is our two-week Jumpstart program. And it's the meals our clients eat in the Jumpstart program that form the heart of this cookbook—so you can try the program out, and see and feel the results. (Those recipes are marked in the table of contents and on the recipes themselves with this image: ❧.)

During our jumpstarts and culinary education classes, it became clear to us that creating a cookbook for the participants would be a perfect addition to our program. The people in our program had diets that were very traditional, and switching to a plant-based diet can feel like a huge change, especially at first. I wanted to provide familiar flavors and recipes that would appeal to entire families, including kids. (We've found that the chances of sticking to a new lifestyle are greatly enhanced if others in the family make the same commitment.) Above all, I wanted to help make plant-based eating both easy and delicious for our Jumpstart clients.

We hoped a cookbook would do the same for those who see *PlantPure Nation* and want to try a plant-based diet, using recipes that are kid-friendly, pleasing to sensitive palates, and diverse in flavors, textures, and spices. I believe plant-based eating should be a pleasure—not just something you do for your health.

Our kids are all grown up now; the oldest is twenty-three and the youngest is seventeen. And the part of our parenting of which I am most proud is the appreciation we instilled in our kids for a plant-based diet. We never took a hard-line approach with our kids when it came to their diets. I simply cooked delicious plant-based meals in our house and always made sure we ate together around the dining room table as a family—the same way my own family did. We educated our kids about the facts of nutrition, inspired by their papa, and ultimately trusted them to embrace a plant-based diet beyond the confines of our cozy home. Being the extreme food police often seems to backfire. Instead, we taught them, modeled the right choices, and helped them practice it.

Research shows that frequent exposure to a wide variety of foods will encourage children to become better eaters later in life. Our kids were known to request food such as artichokes, beets, broccolini, Brussels sprouts, acorn squash, fennel, daikon radishes, wild mushrooms, and others that their peers wouldn't have dreamed of eating. Today, all three eat a large variety of plant-based foods. They all know how to cook, and, importantly, how to enjoy the process. That is what I hope for your family, and what I hope this cookbook will help you accomplish.

Many cookbook authors spend a great deal of time providing pages of nutrition information and sharing nonrecipe details. For this one, I've assumed you already know the health benefits, and so instead I have focused on the food. I wanted this book to be, first and foremost, about great recipes and delicious food.

However, I do include a few short information sections, on pantry ingredients, useful tools, substitution tips, and how to keep plant-based eating easy. If you already have experience with plant-based cuisine, you may want to skip these next few sections and go right to the recipes. But if you are new to plant-based cuisine, some of the information may be helpful.

I've also worked with Nelson and others behind *PlantPure Nation* to share with you more information on the film in sidebars spread throughout the book.

What you'll see in this cookbook I've learned through trial and error over the past twenty-five years, and also through talking to and learning from other plant-based chefs and experts. My philosophy as I travel the path of plant-based cooking is simple: never stop trying new things or learning from others, and always share what you have learned.

As you, too, travel this path, you should know that cooking need not be a mechanical process of measuring and combining ingredients and following instructions. Cooking done right is an art. There are infinite combinations of ingredients, just as there are infinite ways of combining the colors from a painter's palette. Most of all, though, remember that cooking is a life-giving act from which you should derive joy. When you serve yourself, family, and friends, you are serving good health on a platter.

Cooking is not just a hobby to me, but a way of life. I love building, creating, and revising recipes. I'm not afraid to make mistakes, and I never limit myself to just one idea. I hope that my recipes will become yours, and that you will take them and adjust them to your family's preferences and your own. These are now your recipes—my gift to you! I wish you many joyful mealtimes with the people you love and abundant health.

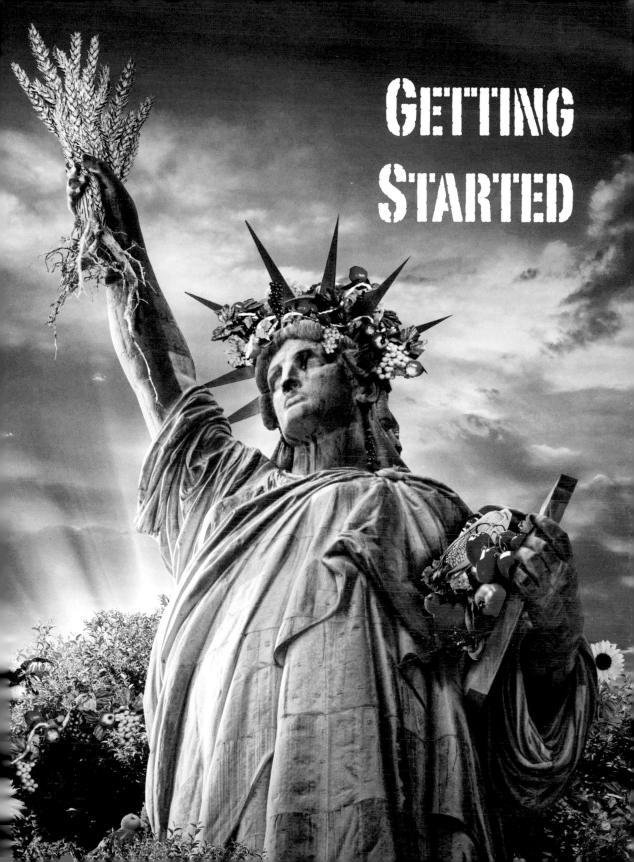

GETTING
STARTED

Building Your PlantPure Pantry

Over the years, I have learned that my best cooking happens when my pantry is filled with a variety of essential spices, beans, sauces, nuts, seeds, flours, and more. For many people, stress in the kitchen happens when you simply don't have the correct ingredients on hand. And switching to a plant-based diet means changing what you think of as pantry staples.

Many of the people I work with want to run out and purchase an entire pantry list immediately. But you don't need to purchase all of these items at once; just try to knock out a little bit each week to build up your pantry. To limit your expense, focus first on the ingredients you need for the recipes you select. Add pantry items as you continue cooking plant-based meals, building your pantry slowly.

There are many products on the market today that are used in plant-based cooking. I have tried to compile an ingredient list of essential items for your pantry connected with the recipes I am sharing in this cookbook, but keep in mind that this is but a subset of a much larger set of possibilities. You should be able to find almost all the ingredients below at a regular supermarket—no specialty or natural food markets required.

BEANS

You can use either canned or dried beans in your cooking, but be aware that dried beans require soaking and cooking for long periods of time. (If you are adamant about using dried beans, then a pressure cooker is a good investment; see more in "Helpful Cooking Tools," page 24.)

Black beans
Black-eyed peas
Cannellini beans/white kidney beans
Chickpeas/garbanzos
Great Northern beans/navy beans
Lentils (green, red, yellow, split pea)
Pinto beans
Red kidney beans

GRAINS, FLOURS, AND OTHER GRAIN PRODUCTS

Store grains and flours in airtight containers in a cool, dark cupboard or other storage unit. An important note: resist the temptation to purchase large quantities of flour. If you purchase more than what you will need you may end up with flour that goes rancid.

Barley: Barley is a member of the grass family. It has a nutty flavor and a chewy, pasta-like consistency, and is high in protein and fiber. I like to use it in soups and stews for a bulkier texture.

Brown Rice: The main difference between brown rice and white rice is that the bran has not been removed from brown rice. Brown rice is much healthier, with more fiber, nutrients, and necessary fatty acids, and has a nuttier flavor and a chewier texture.

The shape of the rice has much to do with its starch content. Long-grain rice is less sticky and often used in pilafs. Medium-grain rice is relatively sticky and used in paellas and risottos. Short-grain rice is the stickiest kind, and I like to use this rice for sushi. I always suggest that new plant-based eaters try short-grain rice if they are used to the texture of white rice. Our family loves stickier rice, so I almost always use short-grain brown rice.

Bulgur wheat: Bulgur wheat is a whole-grain wheat that has been partially cooked, dried, and then cracked. It has a nutty flavor and a chewy texture. I like to use it in stews and dishes where ground beef is usually used. Bulgur cooks quickly and more than doubles in size when cooked.

Cornmeal: This grain is used primarily for cornbread, grits, muffins, and polenta. Cornmeal comes in different textures ranging from coarse to fine. It also comes in white, yellow, and blue varieties. Medium and fine grains are most often used in baking, while coarse grains are used for grits and polenta.

Couscous: Couscous is a wheat product similar to pasta and is a staple in Moroccan cuisine. It cooks quickly and can be found in both white and whole wheat forms.

Oats: Oats are high in protein and fiber and rich in vitamins and minerals. Oats are gluten free and come in many forms: whole oat groats, oat bran, oat flakes, and oat flour.

Pasta: Pasta comes in many shapes, colors, sizes, and even flavors. I recommend only 100 percent whole-grain pastas: whole wheat or brown rice pasta. Whole wheat pasta has a firmer texture and a nuttier flavor, but I prefer brown rice pasta because it is less grainy, cooks quicker, and is gluten free.

Please remember that a pasta is not 100 percent whole wheat if one of the first two ingredients says "enriched." That means the bran has been removed and replaced with artificial vitamin and mineral supplementation.

Quinoa (white, red): Quinoa is a small, round grain that is brown to gold in color. It is an excellent source of protein, containing the ideal balance of amino acids. When cooked it remains granular and has a nutty flavor. Quinoa can be used in place of rice or pasta in most dishes and cooks quickly.

Spelt flour: This grain is an ancient member of the wheat family but is popular among the gluten-sensitive crowd. Spelt flour contains less gluten than modern wheat flour and can be substituted for it in most recipes. It is also lower in fiber and higher in protein than modern wheat flour, which makes it easier to digest.

Vital wheat gluten: This is the protein derived from wheat after the starch is removed. Cooks often use this in breads to make a more uniform loaf. Vegans love to use this in burgers and loaves because it holds the ingredients together like glue. Seitan, for example, is nothing more than water, gluten, and seasonings.

Though I've listed vital wheat gluten here, I use little of it in my cookbook because I find it to be highly processed and refined. Gluten is also hard to digest for many people.

White whole wheat flour: This is a whole-grain flour that comes from a variety of wheat that is golden rather than red, which gives the flour a lighter color. This flour gives a lighter texture to breads and baked goods.

Whole wheat flour: This flour is made from 100 percent whole wheat berries.

Whole wheat pastry flour: Pastry flour is ground from soft wheat berries as opposed to the hard wheat berries used for regular whole wheat flour. Whole wheat pastry flour has less gluten and protein than regular whole wheat flour and is much lighter. I use it often for cakes, cookies, pancakes, and most quick breads.

NUTS, SEEDS, AND NUT BUTTERS

Foods from this category can really add to a recipe and enhance sauces. The fat from the nuts helps emulsify ingredients in sauces and dressings. I like to use a handful of nuts in a recipe rather than oil because nuts and seeds are whole foods. But because nuts and seeds are high-fat foods, we need to pay attention to the amount we use in our diets. They are necessary for good health, but the way they are packaged and processed can lead to overconsumption; if you were to eat nuts in their purest form, you would have to be cracking and shelling a great deal. In our house, I keep nuts in the refrigerator for cooking. Rarely do we eat them by the handful.

Nuts
Almonds
Cashews
Peanuts
Pecans
Pine nuts
Walnuts

Seeds
Chia seeds
Flaxseeds (flax meal is ground-up flaxseeds)
Sesame seeds
Sunflower seeds

Nut butters (Make sure the ingredients have no added oils, salts, or sugars. Use sparingly.)
Almond butter
Cashew butter
Sesame seed butter/tahini
Sunflower butter

VINEGARS, CONDIMENTS, AND SAUCES

Vinegars
Apple cider vinegar
Balsamic vinegar
Red wine vinegar
Rice vinegar
White vinegar

Condiments and Sauces
Dijon mustard
Hoisin sauce
Ketchup, all natural
Lemon juice
Lime juice
Liquid smoke
Sriracha (my favorite hot sauce)

Vegan Worcestershire sauce (I like
    Annie's brand)
Yellow mustard

Soy Sauce, Tamari, and Miso Paste

Soy sauce: Soy sauce is a salty brown liquid made from fermented soybeans. There are many varieties of soy sauces available, so experiment with a few. I prefer low-sodium versions for my recipes.

Tamari: Tamari is a salty brown sauce that, like soy sauce, is made from soybeans. It has a smoother, richer flavor than soy sauce because it contains a higher concentration of fermented soybeans.

Miso paste: Miso is a traditional Japanese seasoning paste made from fermented rice, barley, chickpeas, or soybeans. It is used to flavor sauces and spreads and gives a musty flavor to vegan cheeses.

SWEETENERS

It's important to keep consumption of refined sugars to a minimum. All sweeteners (except Medjool dates) are considered refined and should therefore be used sparingly. I recommend agave nectar more often than not because it has a lower glycemic index than most sweeteners. I personally use these products very infrequently and keep desserts to a minimum, though occasional desserts are fine for special occasions.

Agave: Also known as agave nectar, this liquid sweetener is derived from the blue agave plant, which is part of the cactus family. It varies in color from light to dark amber. Agave is 50 percent sweeter than sugar and has a smooth flavor similar to honey.

Maple Syrup: This natural syrup comes from boiling down the sap of maple trees. The flavor is distinctly nutty, roasted, and sweet. I love maple syrup, but it is very expensive.

Medjool dates: This is a dried tree fruit that can be purchased without pits. It has a rich caramel-like flavor. If pureed, it makes the perfect natural sweetener for sauces, smoothies, and baked goods.

Molasses: This is a dark sweet syrup by-product made during the extraction of sugar from sugarcane. It has a strong flavor and should be used carefully because it can quickly overpower the flavor of any recipe to which it's added.

Sucanat: This sweetener has the taste and consistency of brown sugar. It comes from whole unrefined sugarcane that has been freshly cut and crushed. The juice is extracted and heated, and the resulting dark syrup dried to create granules that have the distinct flavor of molasses. I use it as a substitute for brown sugar whenever I bake.

SALT AND SODIUM

Throughout this cookbook there are portions indicated for salt. However, you should keep salt intake to a minimum by salting very lightly. Over time your taste buds will become more sensitive, enabling you to taste more saltiness with less salt.

To further reduce your sodium intake, always rinse beans before using and buy products with low or reduced sodium. Keep in mind that anything you buy prepared is probably heavily salted. When you buy prepared foods you are at the mercy of the food company. Cooking your own food allows you to be in control of your health.

When selecting a salt, consider the type. Sea salt does not go through the refining and bleaching process that table salt does, so it may be a marginally better choice for that reason. But don't be fooled into believing that sea salt has less sodium than table salt. Too much sodium is harmful to your body whether it comes from table salt or sea salt.

DRIED HERBS AND SPICES

Ancho chili powder
Basil
Black pepper
Cayenne powder (red pepper)
Chipotle chili powder (provides a
    smoky flavor)
Chives
Cinnamon, ground
Cloves, ground
Cumin, ground
Curry powder
Dill
Fennel
Garam masala (you can make this,
    see recipe)
Garlic powder
Ginger, ground
Italian seasoning
Mustard, ground
Nutmeg, ground
Old Bay Seasoning
Oregano
Paprika
Parsley

Red pepper flakes
Rosemary
Sage, rubbed
Tarragon leaves
Thyme leaves
Turmeric, ground

TOFU AND TEMPEH

Tofu: Tofu is also called bean curd. It is made by coagulating soy milk and pressing the resulting curds into soft white blocks. Tofu is absorptive and can be marinated to any desired flavor. There are three varieties of tofu:

Extra-firm tofu (great for stir-fries and
    sautéed dishes)
Firm tofu (slightly softer than extra-
    firm tofu, with a higher
    water content)
Silken tofu (soft and creamy, with the
    highest water content; great
    for salad dressings and smoothies)

My advice is to buy extra-firm tofu, which gives you more bang for the buck because it contains less water. A firm tofu can be processed down by adding water to it. I rarely buy anything else.

Tempeh: Tempeh is made by inoculating soybeans with a special bacterium and incubating them for a period of time. A white fluffy mold develops around the beans, holding them together into a cake. I think of tempeh as soybeans in a cake or patty form.

Tempeh has a firm texture and a pleasant nutty flavor. I like the flavored tempeh, especially the smoked varieties, but again, be careful of your sodium intake, since some tempeh, as well as tofu, can have lots of added salt.

MISCELLANEOUS ITEMS

Canned coconut milk: Canned coconut milk can be purchased in either lite or regular fat content. The lite coconut milk is slightly lower in fat only because they add water to the ingredients.

Cornstarch: Cornstarch is a fine powder made out of corn. It is primarily used as a thickener for soups and sauces. It has twice the thickening power as flour and turns clear after cooking.

Corn (and soy) is one of the top foods genetically engineered, which means the genetic material of the plant has been altered in a way that does not occur naturally. There is growing evidence that foods that have been genetically modified are linked to health problems and environmental hazards. Many countries around the world have restricted and banned the use of genetically modified organisms (GMOs). I highly recommend you buy non-GMO products.

Ener-G Egg Replacer: Ener-G Egg Replacer is a dry product made from mainly potato starch and tapioca flour that has the look and feel of cornstarch or a fine flour. It is used as an egg substitute when preparing baked goods.

Flax meal: Flax meal is simply flaxseeds ground into a flaky powder. When mixed with water, it makes a great egg substitute. It is also great on cereals and mixed into smoothies. Flax meal is high in fiber and rich in nutrients. Store flax meal in the refrigerator or freezer because it has a tendency to go rancid quickly.

Nutritional yeast flakes: Nutritional yeast flakes can be found in the bulk section at most natural food stores. They are rich in B vitamins and protein but low in calories. Nutritional yeast is made of inactive microorganisms and is safe to eat without cooking. It has a mild cheese-like flavor.

Please don't confuse nutritional yeast with brewer's yeast or active dry yeast. Active dry yeast will cause intestinal discomfort and taste terrible.

Seaweed: Seaweed is a great way to bring the flavor of the sea into your dishes. Toasted nori sheets are used for sushi rolls, but I use them whenever I want to add the flavor of "fish" to a dish.

Tomatoes and tomato paste: Typical canned tomatoes are high in sodium, so look for low-sodium brands. I like to buy diced Pomi brand tomatoes that come in a carton, because their sodium content is much lower than that of other brands.

Unsweetened cocoa powder: Cocoa powder is made by pressing chocolate liquor and removing 75 percent of the cocoa butter fat. The solids are then processed and turned into cocoa powder. Unsweetened cocoa powder is bitter and dark, and imparts a rich chocolate flavor to baked goods.

Vegetable stocks: Vegetable stocks can be high in sodium, so I recommend you buy low-sodium versions. Concentrated vegetable stocks, which often come in a jar, are sometimes high in fat and sodium, so it's important to read the ingredients label.

FROZEN PRODUCE

Although frozen foods are not really a pantry item, they are very important foods to have available for easy and quick preparation. Frozen vegetables are the next best thing to fresh vegetables and in many instances better. Fresh vegetables often sit in trucks, in produce racks, and then in our refrigerators for a long time, losing their nutrient quality and freshness along the way. Frozen produce is picked at its peak and flash-frozen immediately. This makes many frozen items more nutritious than their fresher cousins.

Corn
Diced onions
Edamame
Fruits (blueberries, cherries, mangoes, raspberries)
Leeks
Mixed Asian stir-fries
Peas
Roasted mixed peppers
Spinach and greens

Helpful Cooking Tools

Equally important to having a stocked pantry is having the right cooking tools. There is nothing more frustrating than having a great recipe and all your ingredients, then finding that you are lacking an essential tool. Here are the tools that will make your job of preparing the recipes in this cookbook easier.

Food processor: This comes in handy for many of the recipes in this cookbook. Cutting, chopping, shredding, and whipping can all be done in the food processor. This appliance is a must!

Knives and cutting boards: Sharp knives and a few different-sized cutting boards are always the first items I pull from the cupboard in preparing for dinner. Not only do they help get the job done, but using a sharp knife and proper technique can also help prevent nasty cuts.

Pressure cooker: If you like to cook with dried beans and whole grains, this gadget is a great buy, because it cooks everything much faster. Cooking is more pleasant when you can create your masterpiece without having to stand around for a long time waiting for something to cook.

Slow cooker: A slow cooker is essential for those super easy-to-cook meals that you turn to when you don't have the time for anything else. Many times after a busy day at school, I came home to a slow cooker stew, and all I had to do to finish dinner was make a salad and cook some rice.

Vitamix blender: People always cringe when I say this because a Vitamix is expensive. Mine is a refurbished one that I received more than five years ago and it still works like a dream. I'm a cook, so I find myself using it at least once daily, if not two or three times. It will truly turn almost anything into a cream, so it's wonderful to use for dressings, sauces, and soups. I have tried other blenders and nothing compares. Having said this, you can use other blenders; just understand that they may require more soaking and pre-chopping of ingredients.

Making Substitutions

Learning how to "veganize" a recipe is important because the people you're cooking for, especially if they're new plant-based eaters, may still crave traditional comfort foods. Sometimes you simply can't make a replacement (try making a pot roast with plants), or the recipe just flops. However, most of the time, a recipe can be easily changed. Over the years I have learned a few tricks and received advice from the pros. Here are just a few.

Eggs

Eggs are used in recipes to emulsify, bind, leaven, and give structure. Here are a few suggestions for egg replacement.

- 1 tablespoon flax meal plus 3 tablespoons water (let it sit so it thickens)
- 1½ teaspoons Ener-G whisked with 2 tablespoons water
- ¼ cup fruit puree such as applesauce or prune paste

Cheese

Cheese is loaded with saturated fats and with casein, the milk protein that research has linked to cancer and disease. Cheese is often hard to replace, but there are a few alternatives.

Fake vegan cheese is an option, but I use very little of these products. In my work with my husband, we have used sparing amounts in our jumpstarts because our participants are typically new to a plant-based diet. At home, I use vegan cheeses mainly when we have nonvegan guests. These products are loaded with oils, so I'm not sure I approve of this as a staple in the diet.

To replace ricotta: One of the recipes in this cookbook is a tofu ricotta recipe that tastes even better than real ricotta.

To replace Parmesan: Grind up walnuts, bread crumbs, and nutritional yeast using equal ratios.

To replace cheese sauce: I have included in this cookbook recipes for a cauliflower Alfredo sauce that is delicious and a macaroni and no-cheese sauce that works well if you are looking for a nacho sauce or a sauce to pour over veggies. You can even make some ahead of time and store it in the refrigerator.

Milk

This is probably the easiest ingredient to substitute because there are so many choices available. Our house is partial to soy and almond milks, though I had to try many varieties on my kids before we found what worked.

Here are the milk substitutes I recommend:

Almond milk
Hemp milk
Oat milk
Rice milk
Soy milk

OILS AND BUTTERS

Although oils are vegan, we use absolutely no oils in our house. That is not to say we don't consume oil in our plant foods, because we do. We just don't ingest refined oils—that means olive, sesame, canola, corn, and others. Oil is oil and research like the research done by my father-in-law suggests that they are all unhealthy. We can get all the fat we need if we are eating a whole food plant-based diet.

Applesauce: Applesauce is a good replacement in cookies and quick bread.

Avocados: An avocado can be a butter replacement that will add natural fat and creaminess to just about anything.

Bananas: Bananas are a perfect replacement for fats in cookies or quick breads. But be forewarned: unlike cookies and breads made with applesauce, which doesn't add a strong flavor, those made with bananas will taste like bananas!

Nut butters: I use nut butters in my cookies as a fat replacer. They work perfectly.

Prune puree: A thick puree made from pitted prunes and a little bit of water is a great substitute for butter when baking.

Vegetable stock: I use this to sauté my vegetables—though if vegetable stock is not available, water is also a good option.

MEATS

I am not a fan of textured vegetable proteins because they often contain isolated soy proteins. I particularly recommend you stay away from these fake meat products because they are very processed, loaded with oils, and hard to digest. Here are some approved meat substitutes.

Bulgur: When added to soups, stews, marinara sauces, and salads, this grain's texture is similar to that of hamburger. You can season bulgur with any flavor. I like to add taco seasoning and use it as a filling in tacos.

Flavored tempeh: The "fakin' bacon" flavor of tempeh makes it a great replacement for bacon. It's very salty, however, so you may want to rinse it a little before cooking and limit its use.

Frozen and thawed tofu: Freezing and then thawing tofu gives it a more meat-like texture. I freeze tofu prior to marinating so it takes on this firmer texture.

Keeping PlantPure Eating Simple

Cooking plant-based cuisine can be a joyful experience on many levels. But as soon as this lifestyle becomes too complicated, too time-consuming, or in any other way a chore, the joy begins to fade. This is the biggest reason so many people don't stick with the plant-based diet. Don't be discouraged if dinner is a tomato and avocado sandwich; our best meals are oftentimes the quick and easy ones. So it is important as you embark on this journey to always think about how to live plant-based as simply as possible. As many a philosopher has said, there is freedom in simplicity. Here are a few suggestions:

1. Keep a couple of dips handy in the refrigerator, such as hummus, guacamole, or a bean dip. These can always be used for quick sandwiches and salad toppers.

2. Have some grains and other starches cooked and stored for quick access. This will often make it easier to throw a meal together; you can just mix a grain or starch with your choice of vegetables or salad greens. Baked potatoes, for example, keep nicely in the refrigerator and go perfectly with a salad or mixed vegetables.

3. Keep at least two dressings handy for salads and sandwiches. I prefer to make my salad dressings because my recipes have no added oil and minimal sugars. However, if you prefer to buy them, read the ingredients label to make sure there are no added oils.

4. Keep a variety of raw nuts, frozen fruits, and oatmeal handy for breakfast. I also use boxed cereal but only cereals that are low in sugar, are 100 percent whole grain, and have no or very minimal vitamin supplementation. In our house, breakfast is always a quick meal that can be put together in 5 minutes, especially on weekdays when we may be in a hurry to get out the door. Weekends are often better for more leisurely, planned breakfasts.

5. Always have fresh fruit and veggies on hand. This will help when you get the snack attack. Try reaching for an orange, a banana, or an apple when you crave something sweet. Or grab celery, broccoli, or peppers and dip them in a dressing when you crave something savory. The more you do this, the less you will want fat-laden brownies, cookies, and potato chips.

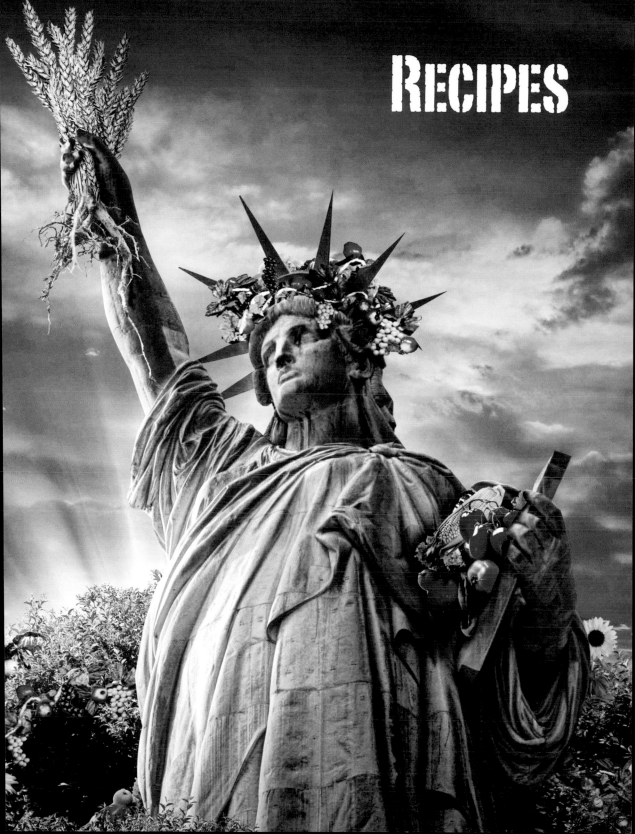

RECIPES

BREAKFAST AND BRUNCH

BAKED APPLES

This recipe is great for breakfast, but it also could be used as a dessert. These freshly baked apples are stuffed with oatmeal, raisins, Sucanat, and spices.

4 apples (Granny Smith or McIntosh)

¼ cup Sucanat

¼ cup dry oats (not instant)

½ teaspoon ground cinnamon

¼ teaspoon ground nutmeg

⅛ teaspoon ground cloves

¼ cup raisins

¼ cup chopped walnuts

½ teaspoon orange zest

Yields: 4 apples
Prep Time: 15 minutes   *Cook Time:* 35 minutes

1. Preheat oven to 375°F. Line a square baking dish with parchment paper and set aside.

2. Remove the cores of the apples, leaving a layer of apple at the bottom to hold the stuffing. This is easy to do with an apple corer but can also be done with a paring knife.

3. Place the apples in the prepared baking dish.

4. In a small bowl, mix the Sucanat, oats, cinnamon, nutmeg, cloves, raisins, walnuts, and orange zest. Divide this mixture among the apples, packing the wells firmly.

5. Bake for 35–40 minutes, or until the apples are tender when poked with a knife.

6. Serve warm.

KIM'S HINTS:
- You can peel the apples if you don't like the skin.
- If coring takes too much time for you, simply slice an apple in half and remove the core, and then you can fill the apple halves by making a bowl shape with each half.
- You can also reduce the amount of Sucanat because apples are naturally sweet.

BLUEBERRY MUFFIN GRANOLA

This is a light granola made with your favorite nut butter and almonds. Dried blueberries give it the perfect sweetness. Serve this over soy yogurt or with your favorite nondairy milk.

4 cups whole-grain dry oats (not instant)

½ teaspoon sea salt

¼ cup Sucanat

½ cup flax meal

1 cup raw blanched almond slivers

½ cup nondairy milk

2 teaspoons vanilla extract

¼ cup unsweetened applesauce

½ cup nut butter (almond, sunflower, or peanut)

¼ cup agave nectar

1 cup dried blueberries

Yields: 6–8 servings
Prep Time: 10 minutes   *Cook Time:* 45 minutes

1. Preheat oven to 300°F. Line a baking sheet with parchment paper and set aside.

2. Mix together the oats, sea salt, Sucanat, flax meal, and almond slivers in a large bowl. Set aside.

3. Whisk together the milk, vanilla, applesauce, nut butter, and agave.

4. Stir the wet ingredients into the dry ingredients until well combined.

5. Spread the granola evenly on the prepared baking sheet.

6. Bake for 30–45 minutes, stirring every 10 minutes to achieve an even color.

7. Remove from the oven and let cool completely. Stir in the dried blueberries.

8. Serve warm or at room temperature.

KIM'S HINTS:
- You will need to keep a close eye on the granola, stirring frequently and being careful not to overbake.
- I also like to add a variety of dried fruit at the end using whatever I have on hand.

BLUEBERRY SAUCE

This sauce is perfect for pancakes or French toast. It brings back memories of eating breakfast at my husband's house, where my mother-in-law had an assortment of different berry sauces to choose from. Pancakes just aren't complete without berries!

2 cups blueberries (fresh or frozen)

½ cup water, divided

1 cup orange juice

2 tablespoons agave nectar

3 tablespoons cornstarch

½ teaspoon coconut flavoring

¼ teaspoon ground cinnamon

Yields: 4 servings

Prep Time: 5 minutes   *Cook Time:* 12 minutes

1. In a saucepan over medium heat, combine the blueberries, ¼ cup of the water, orange juice, and agave. Stir gently and bring to a boil.

2. In a cup or small bowl, mix together the cornstarch and remaining ¼ cup water.

3. Gently stir the cornstarch mixture into the blueberry sauce. Simmer and stir until thick enough to coat the back of a metal spoon, 3–4 minutes.

4. Remove from the heat and stir in the coconut flavoring and cinnamon. Thin the sauce with water if it is too thick for your liking.

KIM'S HINT: You can replace the blueberries with mixed berries or any other berry that is in season.

BREAKFAST BURRITO

This recipe has the best mix of seasonings, hash browns, and vegetables, all wrapped up in a burrito for the perfect breakfast.

1½ cups frozen hash browns

½ onion, diced

3–4 cloves garlic, minced

1 small poblano pepper, seeded and diced small

½ cup diced red bell pepper

¼ cup low-sodium vegetable stock, for sautéing

¼ teaspoon turmeric powder

1 teaspoon onion powder

1 teaspoon garlic powder

2 tablespoons nutritional yeast flakes

¼ teaspoon black pepper

¼ teaspoon sea salt

2 tablespoons vegan bacon bits

2 tablespoons low-sodium soy sauce

One 14-ounce block extra-firm tofu, drained and crumbled

6 whole wheat tortillas

⅓ cup Daiya Mozzarella Style Shreds (optional)

Yields: 6 burritos
Prep Time: 15 minutes   *Cook Time:* 35 minutes

1. Preheat oven to 350°F. Line a baking sheet with parchment paper and set aside.

2. Place the frozen hash browns on the prepared baking sheet and place in the oven. Bake for 10–15 minutes, until tender and warm but not crispy. Remove hash browns from the oven, keeping the oven heated, and line the baking sheet with new parchment paper.

3. In a skillet over medium-high heat, sauté the onion, garlic, poblano pepper, and bell pepper in vegetable stock until tender.

4. Mix in the dry seasonings and bacon bits until well combined. Stir in the soy sauce and crumbled tofu. Continue cooking for an additional 5 minutes over low heat.

5. In each tortilla, add ½ cup of tofu scramble filling, ¼ cup of cooked hash browns, and a small sprinkle of vegan cheese, if using.

6. Roll the tortilla into a closed burrito, place on the prepared baking sheet seam-side down, and bake in the oven for 15 minutes.

7. Serve hot.

KIM'S HINT: You can use whatever vegetables are in season. I have made these burritos with spinach, kale, mushrooms, and tomatoes. They are so customizable that you will find yourself not using a recipe next time!

BREAKFAST CASSEROLE

This casserole is almost like a vegetable sandwich—but soaked in a creamy, flavorful sauce and baked to perfection. It's similar to a scrumptious breakfast or brunch that you would find at a bed and breakfast. I like to serve this when we have guests because I can make it ahead of time and pop it in the oven the next morning.

3 cups nondairy milk

6 ounces silken tofu

3 tablespoons flax meal

¼ teaspoon ground nutmeg

¾ teaspoon black pepper, divided

½ teaspoon ground mustard

2 teaspoons vegan Worcestershire sauce

2 tablespoons minced garlic

8 ounces mushrooms, sliced

10 ounces spinach, chopped

1 onion, diced

1 red bell pepper, seeded and diced

¼ teaspoon sea salt

12 slices whole wheat bread

8 ounces Lightlife Organic Smoky Tempeh Strips

½ cup Daiya Mozzarella Style Shreds (optional)

Yields: 6 servings
Prep Time: 20 minutes   *Cook Time:* 1 hour

1. Preheat oven to 350°F. Line a 9 × 13 inch casserole pan with parchment paper and set aside.

2. Put the milk in a blender with the tofu, flax meal, nutmeg, ½ teaspoon of the black pepper, mustard, and Worcestershire sauce. Blend until completely smooth and set aside.

3. In a skillet over medium-high heat, sauté the garlic, mushrooms, spinach, onion, and bell pepper in a small amount of water. Season with salt and the remaining ¼ teaspoon pepper.

4. Place 6 slices of bread on the bottom of the prepared pan. You may need to cut the bread slices to fit the pan.

5. Arrange the sautéed vegetables, tempeh strips, and cheese, if using, evenly over the top of the bread. You may have to cut or crumble the tempeh to spread evenly.

6. Pour half the milk mixture over the vegetables and tempeh strips.

7. Cover the vegetables and tempeh with the remaining 6 bread slices. (It looks like you are making a casserole sandwich.)

8. Pour the remaining milk mixture over the top of the casserole. Bake uncovered for about 40 minutes, or until golden brown on top. Let cool for 15 minutes and serve warm.

KIM'S HINT: This recipe can be made ahead of time and not baked. Simply assemble the casserole, cover, refrigerate, and then bake before serving.

BREAKFAST PATTIES

Complete these breakfast patties with shredded potatoes, mushrooms, and peppers. With simple flavors everyone will love, these patties are a great addition to any breakfast.

2 tablespoons flax meal

6 tablespoons water

4 green onions, sliced

7 white button mushrooms, chopped

½ cup diced red bell pepper

3 garlic cloves, minced

¼ cup shredded carrot

1½ cups grated potato

½ cup whole wheat bread crumbs

½ teaspoon sea salt

¼ teaspoon black pepper

½ teaspoon fennel seeds

7 ounces extra-firm tofu, drained and crumbled

2 tablespoons vital wheat gluten

Yields: 6 patties
Prep Time: 15 minutes   *Cook Time:* 30 minutes

1. Preheat oven to 375°F. Line a baking sheet with parchment paper and set aside.

2. Mix the flax meal with the water in a small bowl and set aside until thickened.

3. In a skillet over medium-high heat, sauté the green onions, mushrooms, bell pepper, and garlic in a small amount of water until tender.

4. Place the sautéed vegetables and the remaining ingredients (including the flax mixture) in a large mixing bowl and mix thoroughly.

5. Form the mixture into 6 patties.

6. Bake for 20–30 minutes, or until golden brown.

7. Allow the patties to cool and set before serving.

KIM'S HINT: These patties also freeze very well.

FLUFFY WHOLE WHEAT PANCAKES

These hot, fluffy pancakes are made with whole wheat pastry flour. We like these pancakes with hot cherry sauce or Blueberry Sauce (page 36).

1 cup whole wheat pastry
flour

1 tablespoon Sucanat

2 teaspoons baking powder,
sifted

⅛ teaspoon sea salt

1 cup nondairy milk

2 tablespoons unsweetened
applesauce

Yields: 4 servings
Prep Time: 5 minutes   *Cook Time:* 5–10 minutes

1. Mix all the dry ingredients in a large mixing bowl.

2. In a separate bowl, whisk together the milk and applesauce.

3. Stir the wet ingredients into the dry, being careful not to overmix. Overmixing can lead to tough, gummy pancakes. You will have some lumps, but that's fine.

4. Heat a nonstick griddle pan over medium-high heat. Drop a ¼–½ cup of batter onto the preheated pan.

5. Cook until bubbles appear in the middle of the pancake. Flip and continue cooking for 2–3 minutes.

6. Repeat with the remaining pancake batter.

KIM'S HINTS:

- For a thicker or thinner pancake, simply adjust milk as needed.
- You can also substitute a banana for the applesauce.

GINGERBREAD-BLUEBERRY PANCAKES

A special treat if you love gingerbread, these are perfect for the holidays!

2¼ cups white whole wheat flour

1 tablespoon Sucanat

2 teaspoons baking powder

1 teaspoon ground cinnamon

½ teaspoon ground cloves

½ teaspoon ground ginger

½ teaspoon ground nutmeg

¼ teaspoon sea salt

2½ cups nondairy milk

3 tablespoons molasses

1 cup blueberries (fresh or frozen)

Yields: 6 servings
Prep Time: 10 minutes   *Cook Time:* 5–10 minutes

1. Mix all the dry ingredients in a large mixing bowl.

2. In a separate bowl, whisk together the nondairy milk and molasses.

3. Stir the wet ingredients into the dry, being careful not to overmix. Overmixing can lead to tough, gummy pancakes. You will have some lumps, but that's fine.

4. Gently fold in the blueberries.

5. Heat a nonstick griddle pan over medium-high heat. Drop a ¼–½ cup of batter onto the preheated pan.

6. Cook until bubbles appear in the middle of the pancake. Flip and continue cooking for 2–3 minutes.

7. Repeat with the remaining pancake batter.

KIM'S HINT: For a thicker or thinner pancake, simply adjust milk as needed.

GREEN PEPPER TOFU SCRAMBLE

The turmeric in this scramble gives the tofu that yolk-yellow look, while the peppers and onions add texture and flavor. It's a quick and easy breakfast that goes nicely with a fruit salad and whole-grain bread or grits.

1 onion, diced

1 green bell pepper, seeded and diced medium

½ jalapeño pepper, seeded and minced

¼ cup low-sodium vegetable stock, for sautéing

¼ teaspoon ground turmeric

2 tablespoons nutritional yeast flakes

1 tablespoon garlic powder

¼ teaspoon sea salt

¼ teaspoon black pepper

2 tablespoons low-sodium soy sauce

One 14-ounce block extra-firm tofu, drained and crumbled

3 tablespoons chopped fresh parsley (optional)

Yields: 4 servings
Prep Time: 15 minutes   *Cook Time*: 10 minutes

1. In a skillet over medium-high heat, sauté the onion, bell pepper, and jalapeño pepper in the vegetable stock. Cook for 5 minutes, or until the vegetables become tender.

2. Stir in the spices and soy sauce. Continue cooking for 1–2 minutes longer.

3. Add the crumbled tofu and turn the heat to low. Cook for an additional 1–2 minutes.

4. Remove from the heat and stir in the fresh parsley, if using. Serve immediately.

Hot Cinnamon-Apple Cereal

In this recipe, steel-cut oats are cooked with fresh apples with the perfect blend of seasonings for a hearty, healthy breakfast!

1 cup steel-cut oats

1 cup nondairy milk, plus more for serving

1 cup unsweetened applesauce

1 teaspoon ground cinnamon

⅛ teaspoon ground nutmeg

1 apple, peeled, cored, and diced small

2 tablespoons Sucanat

1 cup hot water

¼ teaspoon sea salt

1 teaspoon vanilla extract

Berries or other favorite fruits or nuts, for serving (optional)

Yields: 4 servings

Prep Time: 10 minutes   *Cook Time:* 30 minutes

1. Combine all the ingredients in a saucepan over medium heat. Bring to a low simmer and cook for 20–30 minutes, until the oats become tender and the liquid is close to being completely absorbed.

2. Remove from the heat and serve with berries or other favorite fruits, nuts, and additional nondairy milk, if desired.

MUESLI

I like a mixture of grains, nuts, and dried fruits for an easy breakfast. I prefer muesli to traditional processed cereals.

3 cups whole-grain dry oats (not instant)

1 cup wheat or bran flakes

½ cup rye flakes (optional)

¼ cup unsweetened coconut flakes

¼ cup sunflower seeds (raw or roasted)

¼ cup pumpkin seeds

1 cup dried fruit (raisins, blueberries, or cranberries)

½ cup chopped pitted Medjool dates

3 tablespoons flax meal

1 teaspoon ground cinnamon

Yields: 6 servings
Prep Time: 10 minutes   *Cook Time:* 0 minutes

1. Mix all the ingredients and store in a sealed container.

2. Serve muesli with your favorite nondairy milk and fresh fruit.

KIM'S HINT: Any of these ingredients (except the oats) can be replaced or left out. Making a recipe for muesli is easy because I usually dump whatever ingredients I have on hand into a container and shake. You can choose various nuts, dried fruit, flakes, and even spices.

Mushroom Hash Browns

These seasoned hash browns are baked, not fried in oil, for a slightly crispy texture. They're a great addition to any breakfast.

12 ounces frozen hash browns, thawed

1½ tablespoons minced fresh rosemary

1 tablespoon nutritional yeast flakes

2 tablespoons minced garlic

½ teaspoon sea salt, plus more as needed

¼ teaspoon black pepper, plus more as needed

1 onion, diced

1 red bell pepper, seeded and diced

10 ounces mushrooms, sliced

¼ cup low-sodium vegetable stock, for sautéing

Yields: 4 servings
Prep Time: 15 minutes   *Cook Time:* 20–30 minutes

1. Preheat oven to 400°F. Line a baking pan with parchment paper and set aside.

2. Toss the hash browns with the rosemary, nutritional yeast, garlic, salt, and pepper.

3. Spread the seasoned hash browns evenly over the prepared baking pan. Bake for 20 minutes, or until tender and golden brown. Some of the potatoes should get crispy.

4. Meanwhile, in a nonstick frying pan over medium-high heat, sauté the onion, bell pepper, and mushrooms in the vegetable stock until tender. Season with salt and pepper.

5. When the hash browns are done baking, place them in the pan with mushrooms, onion, and pepper, and toss briefly over medium heat. Serve warm.

NELSON'S GRITS

After having spent a good part of his childhood in the South, and with a mother who hailed from West Virginia, my husband is a huge fan of grits. It's fun to watch him cook grits because he likes to experiment with flavors and sauces. Here is a recipe that we both enjoy.

1 onion, diced

1 jalapeño pepper, seeded and minced

1 poblano pepper, seeded and diced small

1 red bell pepper, seeded and diced

¼ cup low-sodium vegetable stock, for sautéing

4 cups water

1 cup yellow grits

2 tablespoons vegan bacon bits

1 tablespoon nutritional yeast flakes

1 teaspoon garlic powder

½ teaspoon sea salt

¼ teaspoon black pepper

Yields: 4 servings
Prep Time: 15 minutes   *Cook Time:* 20 minutes

1. In a skillet over medium-high heat, sauté the onion, jalapeño, poblano, and bell pepper in the vegetable stock until tender.

2. Add the water and bring to a boil. Slowly add the grits, whisking so the mixture does not form lumps.

3. Turn the heat to low and add the bacon bits and seasonings. Cook until the grits are creamy and thick, 5–10 minutes.

4. Serve warm.

PINEAPPLE-COCONUT SMOOTHIE

This light and refreshing smoothie features coconut milk, bananas, and pineapple.

1 cup cubed pineapple (fresh
   or frozen)

½ cup coconut milk

1 banana

1 cup nondairy milk

½ teaspoon vanilla extract

Yields: 3 servings
Prep Time: 5 minutes   *Cook Time:* 0 minutes

1. Place all the ingredients in a high-powered mixer or blender and process on high speed until smooth and creamy.

2. Serve immediately or chill and save for later.

VANILLA-BERRY SMOOTHIE

This light and refreshing smoothie makes a healthy breakfast drink or snack.

1 cup vanilla soy yogurt

1 cup nondairy milk

1 tablespoon agave nectar

½ teaspoon vanilla extract

1 cup frozen raspberries

¼ cup flax meal

Yields: 3 servings
Prep Time: 10 minutes   *Cook Time:* 0 minutes

1. Place all the ingredients in a high-powered mixer or blender and process on high speed until smooth and creamy.

2. Serve immediately or chill and save for later.

WATERMELON SMOOTHIE

My last pregnancy was hard mainly because I experienced nausea for the entire nine months. Some Chinese people say that watermelon and ginger help with nausea, so during my pregnancy Nelson would trudge to the store in the winter to look for watermelon, which is not an easy or inexpensive task. I thought it was worth it, though—this smoothie really took care of the nausea! I also love this recipe because during the summer, when watermelon is in season, we always have leftover fruit and this is a great way to use it up.

3 cups chopped watermelon

2 cups strawberries (fresh or frozen)

1 cup orange juice

1 tablespoon grated ginger

Yields: 2–4 servings

Prep Time: 5 minutes   *Cook Time:* 0 minutes

1. Place all the ingredients in a blender and blend on high speed until smooth.

2. Serve immediately or chill and save for later.

THE CHINA STUDY
SOWING THE SEEDS OF REVOLUTION

BY ANY MEASURE, *The China Study* by Dr. T. Colin Campbell and his son Tom is a seminal work. Published in 2004, the book details three decades of Dr. Campbell's research at Cornell University on the correlation between the consumption of animal-based foods such as meat, milk, and eggs and the development of cancer, heart disease, type 2 diabetes, and other chronic conditions. Dr. Campbell found that eating a diet of whole, minimally refined plants, such as vegetables, fruits, grains, legumes, and nuts, can prevent, and in some cases even reverse, many of these diseases. It's what Dr. Campbell and others call a whole food, plant-based diet.

November 15. 2011
Task Force on Childhood Obesity

Colin Campbell speaking to the Kentucky House of Representatives

The China Study's influence on the modern plant-based nutrition movement can't be overstated. It was the first book to lay out the purely *scientific* case for the advantages of a plant-based diet. As a result, it reached an audience far beyond the already converted vegan activists who were once the driving force of the movement.

A Google search on *The China Study* produced an impressive three hundred million hits—evidence that the plant-based snowball is rolling inexorably downhill, growing ever bigger by the minute. And *The China Study* is right at its core, and the reason many people see Dr. Campbell as the science father of the plant-based nutrition movement.

NATIONAL BESTSELLER

"Everyone in the field of nutrition science stands on the shoulders of Dr. Campbell, who is one of the giants in the field. This is one of the most important books about nutrition ever written – reading it may save your life."
– *Dean Ornish, MD*

THE MOST COMPREHENSIVE STUDY OF NUTRITION EVER CONDUCTED

—THE—
CHINA STUDY

STARTLING IMPLICATIONS FOR DIET, WEIGHT LOSS AND LONG-TERM HEALTH

T. COLIN CAMPBELL, PhD
AND THOMAS M. CAMPBELL II, MD

FOREWORD BY JOHN ROBBINS, AUTHOR, *DIET FOR A NEW AMERICA*

BREADS

Artisanal Vegan Pizza Dough

I prefer to bake my pizzas on a pizza stone. This allows the crust to become light and crispy, as if it had been cooked in a wood-burning pizza oven. Homemade pizza crust is time-consuming, but this recipe has been tested to perfection. It's well worth the effort.

1 tablespoon active dry yeast

1 cup warm water

¼ cup agave nectar

¾ cup nondairy milk

1¾ teaspoons Ener-G Egg Replacer mixed with 1 tablespoon water

1½ teaspoons sea salt

2¼ cups whole wheat flour

¾ cup white whole wheat flour

Yields: Two 14- to 15-inch crusts
Prep Time: 15 minutes
Cook Time: 1 hour 45 minutes (includes rising)

1. In a large bowl, dissolve the yeast in the warm water. Let stand until frothy.

2. Stir in the agave, milk, egg replacer mixture, salt, and flours to make a soft dough. Knead for 6–8 minutes, until smooth.

3. Place the dough in a bowl and cover with a damp towel. Set aside in a warm place to rise, until the dough doubles in size, about 1 hour.

4. Punch down the dough and allow to double in size again, about 30 minutes.

5. During the second rise, preheat oven to 450°F.

6. Divide the dough in half. On a floured cutting board, roll out each half into a ¼-inch-thick crust. Place the crusts on a pizza pan or stone. Evenly poke the pizza dough with a fork.

7. Bake for 4–6 minutes, until just beginning to brown.

8. To make pizzas, top the crusts with the desired sauces and toppings.

9. Return the pizzas to the oven for another 10–15 minutes, until the sauces and toppings are done to your liking and the crusts are golden brown around the edges, and serve warm.

Banana Bread

This is an unusual yeast bread because most banana breads are leavened with baking powder. I think this bread is lighter, less sweet, and more flavorful than typical quick banana breads. It requires more time to rise, but if you are home, it's well worth the wait.

1 cup nondairy milk, warm

¼ cup agave nectar

1½ teaspoons active dry yeast

2 ripe bananas

1½ teaspoons vanilla extract

1 teaspoon ground cinnamon

½ teaspoon ground nutmeg

2½ cups white whole wheat flour

¼ teaspoon sea salt

½ cup chopped walnuts

Yields: 6 servings
Prep Time: 15 minutes
Cook Time: 2 hours 15 minutes (includes rising)

1. Line a bread pan with parchment paper. Silicone bread pans work nicely, too.

2. In a medium bowl, whisk together the warm nondairy milk, agave, and yeast. Let this mixture sit for 10 minutes so the yeast activates.

3. Mash the bananas in a separate bowl (you should have a little over a cup of banana puree) and mix in the vanilla, cinnamon, and nutmeg. Whisk the banana mixture into the yeast mixture.

4. Slowly add the flour and salt and mix for 2 minutes. Add the walnuts. The dough will be very sticky, so kneading is not possible or necessary!

5. Scoop the dough into the prepared bread pan.

6. Cover with plastic wrap and let rise for 90 minutes.

7. While the dough is rising, preheat the oven to 375°F.

8. Uncover the bread and bake for 45 minutes to 1 hour, until an inserted toothpick comes out clean. Tent with aluminum foil after about 20 minutes to keep the top from browning too much.

9. Remove from the oven and cool for 15 minutes, then turn out onto a cooling rack.

10. Cool the bread completely before slicing.

COLIN'S BLUEBERRY MUFFINS

My son, Colin, loved these muffins, especially with breakfast. These also were a favorite after-school snack in my house.

1 tablespoon flax meal

3 tablespoons warm water

¾ cup nondairy milk

½ cup applesauce

3 tablespoons agave nectar

2 cups whole wheat pastry flour

1 tablespoon baking powder

¼ teaspoon sea salt

1 cup blueberries (fresh or frozen)

½ cup chopped walnuts

Yields: 12 muffins
Prep Time: 10 minutes   *Cook Time:* 20 minutes

1. Preheat oven to 400°F.

2. Combine the flax meal and warm water in a small bowl and set aside.

3. In a separate large bowl, mix the milk, applesauce, and agave. When the flax meal and water has thickened, add it to the milk mixture and stir to combine.

4. Stir in the flour, baking powder, and salt all at once. Only mix until the flour is moistened (the batter will be lumpy).

5. Gently fold in the blueberries and chopped walnuts.

6. Using a silicone muffin pan, divide the batter among the muffin cups. Bake for 15–20 minutes, or until golden brown.

CORNBREAD

This bread is slightly sweet and very moist. It goes well with a bowl of chili or Mexican-style salads.

1 tablespoon Ener-G Egg Replacer

2 tablespoons warm water

2 cups finely ground cornmeal

2 teaspoons baking powder

⅛ teaspoon sea salt

1½ cups soy milk

¼ cup applesauce

2 tablespoons agave nectar

Yields: 8 servings
Prep Time: 10 minutes   *Cook Time:* 20 minutes

1. Preheat oven to 375°F. Line a 9 × 9 inch square pan with parchment paper and set aside.

2. In a small bowl, mix the egg replacer with the water. Set aside.

3. In a large bowl, whisk together the cornmeal, baking powder, and salt.

4. Add the milk, applesauce, agave, and egg replacer mixture to the large bowl.

5. Pour the batter into the prepared pan and bake for about 20 minutes, until a toothpick inserted into the center comes out clean. Serve warm.

KIM'S HINT: I like to add finely diced jalapeños and fresh corn to this recipe for a heartier, spicier version.

CRANBERRY-ORANGE SCONES

My biggest weakness is a scone from Starbucks or Barnes & Noble. I think this was the last animal-based product I gave up. At times, I have been known to fall off the wagon and find one in my hand.

For my birthday, my daughter Laura made cranberry-orange scones, and they're worth sharing. This recipe is a healthier version, but the scones are rich, so I consider them a treat.

2½ cups whole wheat pastry flour, plus more as needed

¼ cup Sucanat

1 tablespoon baking powder

½ teaspoon sea salt

1¼ cups coconut milk, cold

¼ cup unsweetened applesauce

1 cup cranberries (fresh or dried)

2 teaspoons orange zest

2 tablespoons natural granulated sugar, for garnish (optional)

Yields: 8 scones

Prep Time: 10 minutes   *Cook Time:* 20 minutes

1. Preheat oven to 425°F. Line a baking sheet with parchment paper and set aside.

2. In a large mixing bowl, combine the flour, Sucanat, baking powder, and salt. Pour in the coconut milk and applesauce.

3. Gently mix until everything is combined, being careful not to overmix. Overmixing can make your scones tough.

4. Gently fold in the cranberries and orange zest. You may need a bit more flour if your dough is very wet. However, too much flour will make your scones dry.

5. Transfer the dough to a floured surface and shape into a disk about 10 inches in diameter and about 1 inch thick. I use my hands to shape it.

6. Using a sharp knife, cut into 8 wedges, like you would with a pizza.

7. Using a spatula, place the wedges onto the prepared baking sheet. Sprinkle the scones with a small amount of the natural sugar.

8. Bake for 15–20 minutes, or until golden. Serve immediately for best results.

NAAN BREAD

This Indian-style flatbread can be made ahead and frozen. Its slightly sweet flavor makes it an excellent bread for sandwiches or for dipping. Naan bread is easy to make but requires some time for kneading, rising, and rolling.

1 tablespoon active dry yeast

1 cup warm water

⅓ cup agave nectar

¾ cup unsweetened soy milk

2¼ teaspoons Ener-G Egg Replacer mixed with 1 tablespoon water

½ teaspoon garlic powder

1 teaspoon rice vinegar

1½ teaspoons sea salt

4 cups whole wheat flour, more or less as needed

Yields: 18–20 pieces
Prep Time: 15 minutes
Cook Time: 68 minutes (includes rising)

1. In a large bowl, dissolve the yeast in the warm water. Let stand until frothy.

2. Stir in the agave, soy milk, egg replacer mixture, garlic powder, vinegar, salt, and flour to make a soft dough. You may have to add more or less flour depending on the type of flour you use. Do NOT use pastry flour because it will produce a gummy dough.

3. Turn out onto a lightly floured surface and knead for 6–8 minutes until smooth. Place the dough in a bowl and cover with a damp towel. Set aside in a warm place to rise until doubled in size, about 1 hour.

4. Punch down the dough and then pinch the dough into 18–20 small nectarine-size balls. Place on a dry tray and allow to double in size, about 30 minutes.

5. Preheat a griddle pan over medium-high heat. On a work surface next to the griddle, roll out one of the dough balls and stretch out the dough to form an uneven roundish shape.

6. Place on the griddle. Cook for 2–3 minutes, until puffy and lightly golden. Do not overcook; you want them to be able to fold without cracking. Turn over and cook the other side.

7. Continue to make all the naan until finished. Naan bread freezes well.

No-Knead Sweet Raisin Bread

This recipe is very similar to the Whole Wheat Sandwich Bread (page 71), except it's slightly sweeter and makes a great breakfast bread. It's delicious with peanut butter and jelly, too.

1½ cups warm water

¼ cup orange juice

¼ cup unsweetened applesauce

3 tablespoons molasses

2 teaspoons active dry yeast

3 cups white whole wheat flour

1 teaspoon sea salt

1½ teaspoons ground cinnamon

1 cup raisins

Yields: 1 loaf
Prep Time: 15 minutes
Cook Time: 2 hours 15 minutes (includes rising)

1. Line a bread pan with parchment paper and set aside.

2. In a small mixing bowl, whisk together the warm water, orange juice, applesauce, molasses, and yeast. Let stand for 10 minutes so the yeast activates.

3. In a large mixing bowl, mix together the flour, salt, and cinnamon.

4. Add the wet ingredients to the dry ingredients and mix the dough vigorously for about 3 minutes. Add the raisins during this time. You should have a very sticky dough. It won't pour, but it will not be kneadable.

5. Scoop the dough into the prepared bread pan. Cover the pan with plastic wrap and let rise in a warm place for 90 minutes.

6. While the dough is rising, preheat oven to 350°F.

7. Uncover the bread and bake for about 45 minutes, tenting it with aluminum foil after 20 minutes to keep the top from browning too much.

8. Remove from the oven and let cool for 15 minutes, then turn out onto a rack. Cool the bread completely before slicing.

KIM'S HINT: You can buy silicone bread pans, which don't need to be oiled or lined with parchment paper. Amazon and kitchen supply stores carry several silicone pans to choose from.

Whole Wheat Sandwich Bread

This recipe is oil-free and requires no kneading! I gave away my bread machine after I started making this recipe.

2 cups warm water

2 tablespoons agave nectar

⅓ cup unsweetened applesauce

1½ teaspoons active dry yeast

3½ cups whole wheat flour

1 teaspoon sea salt

Yields: 1 loaf
Prep Time: 15 minutes
Cook Time: 2 hours 15 minutes (includes rising)

1. Line a bread pan with parchment paper and set aside.

2. In a small mixing bowl, whisk together the warm water, agave, applesauce, and yeast. Let stand for 10 minutes so the yeast activates.

3. In a large mixing bowl, whisk together the flour and salt. Add the wet ingredients to the dry ingredients and mix the dough vigorously for about 3 minutes. You should have a very sticky dough. It won't pour, but it will be too wet to knead.

4. Scoop the dough into the prepared bread pan. Cover the pan with plastic wrap and let rise in a warm place for 90 minutes.

5. While the dough is rising, preheat oven to 350°F.

6. Uncover the bread and bake for about 45 minutes, tenting it with aluminum foil after 20 minutes to keep the top from browning too much.

7. Remove from the oven and let cool for 15 minutes, then turn out onto a rack. Cool the bread completely before slicing.

THE GENESIS OF *PLANTPURE NATION*

NELSON CAMPBELL DREW upon a lifetime of experience in conceiving the idea for *PlantPure Nation*. As the son of world-renowned nutritional biochemist Dr. T. Colin Campbell, Nelson had a front-row seat to one of the greatest scientific discoveries ever made: that a whole food, plant-based diet can prevent, and in some cases reverse, serious illnesses like type 2 diabetes, heart disease, and even some forms of cancer. He also witnessed how difficult it was to bring this discovery to light, mainly because of the opposition it aroused from big special interests like agribusiness. That experience also led Nelson to a career as an entrepreneur in health and wellness and a desire to use the skills he gained to help bring his father's health message into the mainstream.

In early 2012, Nelson worked with Representative Tom Riner to draft and introduce legislation in Kentucky that would have instituted a pilot project to demonstrate the efficacy of a plant-based diet. When that legislation failed to pass, it made him realize that if he did the pilot project successfully on his own, then went back to the Kentucky legislature and showed them how incredible the results were, it could be an opportunity to address the political challenge his father has faced his entire career. He also realized it would make a great storyline for a film. And thus, *PlantPure Nation* was born.

Film crew interviewing Kentucky resident Betsy Coffee in front of the capitol building

SNACKS AND APPETIZERS

ASIAN SPRING ROLLS

These spring rolls can be an appetizer, a lunch, or a side to any entrée. The rolls are filled with fresh mint, thinly sliced vegetables, and light rice noodles. Feel free to add other vegetables that you enjoy. They are beautiful and easy to assemble once you learn the technique. Practice makes perfect!

This recipe includes a spicy, tangy peanut dipping sauce, but if your time is short there are some great sauces available in most grocery stores that have no added oils.

Dipping Sauce

2 tablespoons natural creamy peanut butter (no added oils)

2 tablespoons rice vinegar

2 teaspoons agave nectar

½ teaspoon red pepper flakes

2 tablespoons water

Filling

1½ ounces bean thread noodles, uncooked

1 tablespoon tahini

Dash of red pepper flakes

½ cucumber, julienned

1 carrot, shredded

½ red bell pepper, seeded and thinly sliced

1 avocado, pitted and thinly sliced

2 green onions, sliced

½ tablespoon rice vinegar

½ teaspoon agave nectar

1 tablespoon lime juice

8 rice paper wrappers

8 small whole leaves romaine lettuce

2 tablespoons cilantro leaves

3 tablespoons mint leaves

Yields: 8 spring rolls
Prep Time: 45 minutes   *Cook Time:* 5 minutes

1. To make the sauce, combine the peanut butter, rice vinegar, agave, red pepper flakes, and water in a small bowl. Mix well and set aside.

2. To make the filling, cook the bean threads according to the package directions. Drain the noodles, put them in a bowl, and toss with the tahini and a dash of red pepper flakes.

3. Combine the cucumber, carrot, bell pepper, avocado, and green onions in a large bowl. Toss the veggies with rice vinegar, agave, and lime juice.

4. To soften the rice wrappers, place warm water in a cake pan. Immerse each wrapper in the hot water until it softens, about 30 seconds. Place the wet wrapper on a plate or clean countertop. Fill the center of the softened wrapper by laying down one small romaine lettuce leaf. Then lay down 1–2 tablespoons of noodles and a small amount of the veggie mixture. Add cilantro and mint leaves.

5. To roll up your rice wrappers, first fold the top and bottom of the edges of the wrapper over the filling, then fold in the edges toward the center and continue rolling until it is closed and snug. Continue this process with each of the wrappers.

6. As you finish each roll, place it on a baking sheet and cover the rolls with a damp towel. If desired, slice each roll in half with a sharp knife, or serve the rolls whole, and serve with the peanut sauce on the side.

KIM'S HINTS:

- I like to think of folding a spring roll as folding a closed burrito. The first time I learned how to make these I used a video on YouTube! The visual instruction was perfect.
- Once you learn how to handle the rice wrappers, you can fill them with a variety of fresh vegetables. I love to use fresh salad greens, baked tofu, and avocado for a quick spring roll.

CAULIFLOWER BUFFALO BITES

These are a crowd-pleaser for any event. Chicken wings are never missed when you can have cauliflower bites. I serve these with celery sticks, carrots, and my plant-based Blue Cheez Dressing (page 125).

1 cup nondairy milk

1 cup whole wheat pastry flour

1 teaspoon garlic powder

½ teaspoon onion powder

⅛ teaspoon black pepper

1 teaspoon paprika

2 tablespoons nutritional yeast flakes

1 cauliflower head, broken into florets

10 ounces oil-free buffalo wing sauce

1 cup Blue Cheez Dressing (page 125)

Carrot sticks, for serving

Celery sticks, for serving

Yields: 6 servings
Prep Time: 15 minutes   *Cook Time:* 20 minutes

1. Preheat oven to 400°F. Line a baking sheet with parchment paper and set aside.

2. In a mixing bowl, whisk together the milk, flour, spices, and nutritional yeast.

3. Place all the cauliflower pieces in the milk mixture and coat thoroughly.

4. Spread the cauliflower on the prepared baking sheet.

5. Bake for 20–30 minutes, or until light golden brown.

6. Once the cauliflower florets are crisp and golden, coat them with the buffalo sauce and bake for an additional 5 minutes.

7. Serve with the Blue Cheez Dressing and carrot and celery sticks.

Mushroom Tapenade on Polenta Squares

If you love olives and mushrooms as much as my family does, you will enjoy this tapenade. Here, it is spread over polenta squares, but it can also be served over bread for a beautiful and tasty appetizer.

1 onion, diced

10 ounces button
   mushrooms, sliced

4 ounces shiitake
   mushrooms, sliced

4 garlic cloves, minced

1 teaspoon dried thyme

¼ teaspoon sea salt

¼ teaspoon black pepper

¼ cup dry white wine

One 6-ounce can pitted black
   olives, drained

2 tablespoons capers, drained
   and rinsed

2 tablespoons chopped fresh
   basil

1 recipe Polenta (page 79)

Yields: 10 servings
Prep Time: 30 minutes   *Cook Time:* 10 minutes

1. In large skillet over medium-high heat, sauté the onion, mushrooms, garlic, thyme, salt, and pepper in a little bit of water for 3–5 minutes, until softened. Stir frequently. Add the wine and cook until absorbed.

2. Transfer the mushroom mixture to a food processor. Add the olives, capers, and basil. Pulse until blended but still chunky.

3. Cut the polenta into 2 × 2 inch squares and top with a spoonful of tapenade.

POLENTA

Polenta is Italian for cornmeal mush. In this recipe, it is cooled and cut into squares.

4 cups water

1⅓ cups polenta cornmeal

½ teaspoon garlic powder

3 tablespoons nutritional yeast flakes

½ teaspoon sea salt

¼ teaspoon black pepper

Yields: 6 servings
Prep Time: 5 minutes   *Cook Time:* 15–20 minutes

1. Line a baking sheet with parchment paper and set aside.

2. Bring the water to a slow simmer in a pot over medium heat.

3. Slowly stir in the cornmeal, about ¼ cup at a time. Cook over low heat for 15 minutes, stirring frequently and scraping the bottom to avoid burning.

4. The cornmeal is done cooking when it is smooth and thick. Stir in the remaining ingredients before removing from the heat.

5. Press the polenta into the prepared baking sheet until it is 1 inch thick.

6. Refrigerate until completely cool.

7. Slice the polenta into the desired shape and top with your favorite sauce or vegetable sauté.

KIM'S HINTS:

- Polenta takes on the flavors you give it. You can season with different herbs for unique flavors. After you slice the polenta, you can also bake or grill the slices for a roasted texture.
- To save time, you can purchase premade polenta in the grocery store (they sell a variety of flavors). Then your only task is to prepare the tapenade.

POPCORN, MANY FLAVORS

Popcorn is a healthy and fun snack that goes well with any movie. But it can be oily and extremely unhealthy when purchased at the theater or eaten out of a microwave bag. So try this version!

½ cup unpopped popcorn
   kernels

Seasoning Combinations

Traditional:
  2 tablespoons nutritional
  yeast flakes, 1 teaspoon
  sea salt

Indian:
  ½ teaspoon curry powder,
  ½ teaspoon Garam Masala
  (page 146), ¼ teaspoon
  chili powder, ⅛ teaspoon
  ground cinnamon,
  1 teaspoon sea salt

Italian:
  1 teaspoon dried basil,
  1 teaspoon dried parsley,
  ½ teaspoon garlic powder,
  1 tablespoon nutritional
  yeast flakes, 1 teaspoon
  sea salt, ½ teaspoon black
  pepper

Cajun/Creole:
  1 teaspoon Old Bay
  Seasoning, ½ teaspoon
  dried lemon zest,
  1 teaspoon sea salt

Mexican:
  2 teaspoons Mrs. Dash
  Southwest Chipotle
  Seasoning Blend or
  Mexican Spice Blend
  (page 147), 1 teaspoon
  sea salt

Yields: 4 servings or 14–15 cups popcorn
Prep Time: 5–10 minutes   *Cook Time:* 2–5 minutes

1. Microwave popcorn: Add ½ cup of the popcorn kernels to a large brown lunch bag and fold the top a few times to keep the popcorn from popping out and making a mess. Microwave on high for about 2 minutes or until the popping slows. Repeat with the remaining popcorn. Note that cook times may vary depending on your microwave.

2. Air-popped popcorn: You will need to purchase a fairly inexpensive hot air popper that usually runs about $20. It's worth the investment if you love popcorn and don't want all the fat. Follow the manufacturer's directions. Note that cook times may vary depending on your hot air popper.

3. Seasoning: Flavor the popcorn with spices when the popcorn is hot, because this will help the spices stick to the surface. Use a very fine sea salt.

> **KIM'S HINT:** Put Bragg's Liquid Aminos or a vinegar (depending on what you like) in a spray bottle and lightly spray the popcorn. A light mist will help your seasonings stick. Be careful not to spray too much or your popcorn will become soggy.

POTATO CHIPS

These chips are a fantastic, healthy alternative to store-bought brands. You have total control of sodium and oil intake. The chips take a little more time to prepare and bake, but they are truly delicious!

4 yellow potatoes
1 teaspoon sea salt

Yields: 4 servings
Prep Time: 20 minutes   *Cook Time:* 15–20 minutes

1. Preheat oven to 400°F. Line a baking sheet with parchment paper and set aside.

2. Clean each whole potato and cut into ⅛-inch-thick slices. Try to keep each slice consistent in size to prevent some chips from cooking faster than others.

3. Place the sliced potatoes in cold water to prevent browning and remove excess starch. Let stand in the cold water for 20–30 minutes.

4. Pat the potato slices dry and lay the potato slices in a single layer on the prepared baking sheet. Sprinkle the potatoes with the salt and place in the oven.

5. Bake for 15–20 minutes, or until crisp. This really varies depending on the thickness of your potatoes. I keep a close eye on the potatoes, tossing them every 5–6 minutes if necessary. They can turn from golden brown to black quickly. The first time you make them, I recommend that you keep a close eye on the potatoes and discover the best cook time for your oven.

6. Serve warm out of the oven or cool completely and store in an airtight container.

> **KIM'S HINT:** I recommend using a mandoline slicer for the potatoes. This will give you thin, evenly cut potatoes. However, it is not a necessity, since I have made this recipe often without a mandoline slicer, but cutting is a bit more tedious.

Dips and Spreads

BABA GHANOUSH

This Middle Eastern dip is made with mashed roasted eggplant blended with tahini, chickpeas, lemon juice, and seasonings. It's a perfect spread or dip to complement fresh vegetables and breads.

1 eggplant

One 15-ounce can chickpeas, rinsed and drained

3 garlic cloves

¼ cup lemon juice

3 tablespoons tahini

½ teaspoon sea salt

¼ cup water

2 tablespoons chopped parsley

Servings: 6
Prep Time: 10 minutes   *Cook Time:* 45 minutes

1. Preheat oven to 400°F. Line a baking sheet with parchment paper and set aside.

2. Slice the eggplant in half lengthwise and poke the skin of each half with a fork about 10 times. Lay the eggplant halves on the prepared baking sheet with the skin side facing up. Roast in the oven for approximately 45 minutes, or until the skins become soft and wrinkly.

3. Remove the eggplant from the oven and allow to cool slightly. Scoop out the inside of the eggplant (pulp) with a spoon, discarding the skin.

4. In a blender or food processor, combine the eggplant pulp, chickpeas, garlic, lemon juice, tahini, and salt until smooth. The mixture will be somewhat thick.

5. Add the water slowly until you have your desired consistency. Adjust the amount of water as needed for a thicker or thinner consistency.

6. Mix in the chopped parsley by hand. Best served fresh.

BASIL-AVOCADO PESTO

Pesto is great on pasta, sandwiches, pizza, and salads. There are many versions of pesto, but they all begin with a handful of fresh basil and pine nuts. I've tried so many vegan pestos, but many of them unfortunately contain large amounts of olive oil. This pesto, without added oils, is rich, creamy, and bursting with flavor.

2 cups fresh basil

¼ cup pine nuts

2 tablespoons lemon juice

3 garlic cloves

½ teaspoon sea salt

2 tablespoons nutritional yeast flakes

Dash of cayenne pepper

⅛ teaspoon black pepper

1 fresh avocado, pitted and peeled

2 tablespoons water, if needed

Yields: 4–6 servings
Prep Time: 10 minutes   *Cook Time:* 0 minutes

1. Combine all the ingredients in a food processor, Vitamix, or other high-powdered blender until smooth.

2. If you like a thinner pesto, simply add more water.

KIM'S HINTS: Try replacing the pine nuts with walnuts, pecans, or cashews. Or add 5–6 ounces of silken tofu for a creamy pesto sauce. You can also replace the basil with cilantro to make cilantro pesto.

CHICKPEA-CRANBERRY SALAD

This is a great sandwich filling that doesn't rely on mayonnaise but uses a tahini dressing instead. It's colorful and rich with veggies and herbs. Serve on your favorite bread as a closed or an open-faced sandwich or on a bed of leafy greens. You may even opt to simply enjoy the salad by itself.

¼ cup tahini

¼ cup rice vinegar

¼ cup water

2 tablespoons agave nectar

½ teaspoon dried dill weed

¼ teaspoon red pepper flakes

Two 15-ounce cans chickpeas, rinsed and drained

½ cup diced celery

1 carrot, diced small or shredded

½ cup dried cranberries

½ cup finely chopped walnuts

½ cup diced red onion

¼ cup chopped fresh parsley

¼ teaspoon sea salt

¼ teaspoon black pepper

Yields: 6 servings

Prep Time: 15 minutes   *Cook Time:* 0 minutes

1. Start by mixing your dressing. In a small bowl, combine the tahini, vinegar, water, agave, dill, and red pepper flakes. Set aside so the flavors come together. You can play with the flavor of vinegar you like. I like rice vinegar because it's mild.

2. In a medium to large bowl, add the chickpeas and roughly mash with a strong fork or potato masher.

3. Add the celery, carrot, cranberries, nuts, red onion, parsley, salt, pepper, and tahini dressing. Mix well.

4. Serve at room temperature or let chill in the refrigerator for an hour before serving.

GUACAMOLE

Avocados are pureed to a creamy consistency and combined with tomatoes, onions, and cilantro in this tasty guacamole.

2 avocados, pitted and peeled

¼ cup peas (fresh or frozen)

2 tablespoons lime juice

1 garlic clove

⅛ teaspoon sea salt

1 teaspoon ground cumin

¼ teaspoon ancho chili powder

¼ cup small-diced red onion

1 tomato, finely chopped

½ jalapeño pepper, seeded and minced

1½ tablespoons chopped cilantro

Yields: 4 servings
Prep Time: 15 minutes   *Cook Time:* 0 minutes

1. In a food processor, combine the avocados, peas, lime juice, garlic, sea salt, cumin, and chili powder. Pulse, leaving visible chunks.

2. Transfer the guacamole to a large bowl and fold in the onion, tomato, jalapeño, and cilantro. Refrigerate for an hour before serving.

Southwestern Black Bean Dip

SOUTHWESTERN BLACK BEAN DIP

This spicy dip is bursting with Mexican flavors. It's great as a dip or sandwich spread.

Two 15-ounce cans black beans, rinsed and drained

2 teaspoons minced chipotle (in adobo sauce)

1 teaspoon ancho chili powder

½ cup low-sodium vegetable stock

2 tablespoons smashed roasted garlic

¼ cup small-diced roasted red bell pepper

¼ cup chopped fresh cilantro

Yields: 4–6 servings
Prep Time: 10–15 minutes   *Cook Time:* 0 minutes

1. Place all the ingredients except the bell pepper and cilantro in a food processor. Process until smooth.

2. Add the bell pepper and cilantro and then pulse slightly. Do not puree the cilantro and peppers.

VEGAN RICOTTA CHEESE

I've been making this recipe for more than twenty years but recently found it packaged under the brand name Tofutti. I was immediately disappointed, however, after checking the ingredients label. It was full of processed oils! This recipe is so easy to make and very versatile. It can be used for calzones, lasagna, stuffed shells, and even pizza.

3 garlic cloves

One 14-ounce block extra-firm tofu, drained

¼ cup nutritional yeast flakes

¼ teaspoon ground nutmeg

½ teaspoon onion powder

¼ teaspoon cayenne pepper

1 tablespoon lemon juice

½ teaspoon sea salt

¼ teaspoon black pepper

Yields: 4–6 servings
Prep Time: 10 minutes   *Cook Time:* 0 minutes

1. Place all the ingredients into a food processor. Blend continuously until smooth and creamy. Store in the refrigerator.

> **KIM'S HINT:** I also like to add basil to give this a mint-green color and the flavor of fresh pesto.

THE KENTUCKY LEGISLATURE

IN NOVEMBER 2011, Kentucky State Representative Tom Riner invited Dr. T. Colin Campbell to give a presentation before the Kentucky House of Representatives on the thirty years of pioneering research he has done into the health benefits of a whole food, plant-based diet.

Tom had been following a plant-based diet ever since he and his wife Claudia bought a copy of Dr. Campbell's seminal book, *The China Study*. Said Tom, "It had a life-transforming impact. Within a month my blood pressure had dropped 25 points, my wife's had dropped 20, my cholesterol had dropped 50. I lost about 30 pounds not trying. And we believe that the Lord allowed us to have a tool to show God's love to others—and that is through helping them regain their health or prevent these chronic diseases that have plagued our state for so many years. Kentucky ranks at the very top of the chart when it comes to heart disease, stroke, and diabetes, as well as the other chronic diseases."

The talk was so well received that Dr. Campbell told his son Nelson about it. Nelson then called Tom. Together, Nelson and Tom collaborated on a piece of legislation that, among other things, would create a pilot project documenting that people could experience dramatic improvements in their health within two weeks of going on a plant-based diet. But once the bill went into committee, it was subjected to the most intense agribusiness lobbying attack Tom had seen in thirty years, and the bill was essentially killed.

Undeterred, Nelson resolved to carry out the pilot project anyway, in his own hometown of Mebane, North Carolina. As he said, "They thought they could kill the idea by killing the bill, but that is hard when the idea is based upon a powerful truth." In the meantime, Tom continued to convert as many of his colleagues as possible by personally going through *The China Study* with them, eventually giving away more than 300 copies of the book.

Both Nelson and Tom's efforts were so successful that they decided to take another shot at the Kentucky House—this time documenting their attempt on film. Instead of instituting a "top down" approach involving the state government, as they had before, they focused on a resolution wherein the government would acknowledge the truth of plant-based nutrition.

Thanks to Tom's thirty years as a Kentucky legislator, the *PlantPure Nation* film team was allowed unprecedented access to interview key members of the Kentucky House of Representatives—including Speaker Greg Stumbo. The result is a dramatic, informative, and inspiring film.

The Kentucky House of Representatives in session at the capitol building

SALADS

ARTICHOKE AND WHITE BEAN SALAD

This is a delicious summertime dish that is full of fresh herbs, beans, olives, and artichokes. It's easy to change the vegetables and try seasonal ones, such as tomatoes, avocados, or cucumbers.

Two 15-ounce cans white beans, rinsed and drained

One 14-ounce jar artichoke hearts (packed in water, not oil), drained and chopped

1 celery stalk, finely diced

1 red bell pepper, seeded and diced

¾ cup chopped black olives

4 green onions, sliced

¼ teaspoon red pepper flakes

½ teaspoon ground fennel seeds

2 tablespoons chopped fresh basil

¼ cup chopped fresh parsley

2 tablespoons lemon juice

¼ cup red wine vinegar

1 teaspoon Dijon mustard

½ teaspoon sea salt

¼ teaspoon black pepper

Yields: 4–6 servings
Prep Time: 15 minutes   *Cook Time:* 0 minutes

1. Place the beans and vegetables into a large mixing bowl.

2. Add the dry seasonings and fresh herbs and stir to combine.

3. In another bowl, mix together the lemon juice, vinegar, and Dijon. Add this mixture to the beans and vegetables and stir to combine.

4. Add salt and pepper, more or less to taste.

BROCCOLI SALAD

This sweet and sour green salad is loaded with colorful veggies, seeds, and raisins. I like to have Tofu Cashew Mayonnaise (page 139) on hand for this salad.

2 broccoli heads, cut into florets

⅓ cup Tofu Cashew Mayonnaise (page 139)

2 tablespoons apple cider vinegar

1 tablespoon agave nectar

4 teaspoons Dijon mustard

1 small red onion, diced small

¼ cup shredded or julienned carrot

½ cup raisins

¼ teaspoon sea salt

⅛ teaspoon black pepper

½ cup sunflower seeds (raw or roasted)

¼ cup vegan bacon bits

Yields: 4 servings
Prep Time: 15 minutes   *Cook Time:* 1 minute

1. Quickly blanch the broccoli florets in boiling water for 20–30 seconds and then shock in ice water. Once the broccoli is cooled, drain and remove the ice.

2. In a large mixing bowl, whisk together the mayonnaise, vinegar, agave, and Dijon. Add the broccoli, onion, carrot, raisins, salt, and pepper and toss well.

3. Garnish with the sunflower seeds and vegan bacon bits.

> **KIM'S HINT:** There are vegan mayonnaises available at Whole Foods and some other supermarkets, but they are rich in refined oil. My Tofu Cashew Mayonnaise is perfect for this recipe.

COLESLAW

This crunchy cabbage and carrot salad is made with Tofu Cashew Mayonnaise (page 139).

6 cups shredded green cabbage

1 carrot, shredded

½ cup sliced green onion

1 red or orange bell pepper, seeded and diced medium

½ cup Tofu Cashew Mayonnaise (page 139)

¼ teaspoon smoked paprika

½ teaspoon black pepper

1 teaspoon celery seed

1 teaspoon onion powder

¾ teaspoon sea salt

2 tablespoons white vinegar

2 tablespoons agave nectar

Yields: 6 servings
Prep Time: 15 minutes   *Cook Time:* 0 minutes

1. In a large bowl, combine the cabbage, carrot, green onion, and bell pepper.

2. Add the mayonnaise, seasonings, vinegar, and agave and toss thoroughly to coat the vegetables with the sauce mixture until well combined.

3. Chill in the refrigerator before serving.

CORN SALSA

This recipe is quick and easy to prepare. The unique flavors of sweet and tangy give this dish a fresh and succulent flavor. It's a garden of vegetables both fresh and colorful!

12 ounces corn (fresh or frozen)

2 red bell peppers, seeded and diced medium

2 jalapeño peppers, seeded and diced small

½ cup small-diced red onion

½ cup chopped fresh cilantro

2 tablespoons lime juice

2 teaspoons agave nectar

½ teaspoon sea salt

Yields: 4–6 servings
Prep Time: 15 minutes   *Cook Time:* 0 minutes

1. If using frozen corn, thaw it.

2. Combine all the vegetables in a bowl, then add the cilantro, lime juice, agave, and salt. Stir to blend well.

3. Let this dish stand for a least an hour to absorb all the flavors before serving.

CREAMY KALE SALAD

Chopped kale, shredded carrots, and red bell peppers marinated in an almond dressing make this dish not only delicious but also nutrient dense. Kale has never tasted so good!

2 bunches curly kale, chopped, with stems removed

2 carrots, shredded

1 red bell pepper, seeded and diced

3 radishes, cleaned and thinly sliced

2 tablespoons lime juice

2 teaspoons pureed ginger

¼ cup almond butter

¼ cup diced onion

¼ cup water

2 garlic cloves

2 teaspoons agave nectar

¼ teaspoon red pepper flakes

¼ teaspoon sea salt

2 tablespoons sunflower seeds (raw or roasted)

Yields: 4 servings
Prep Time: 30 minutes   *Cook Time:* 0 minutes

1. Place the kale, carrots, bell pepper, and radishes in a bowl and toss until mixed. Set aside.

2. In a Vitamix or other blender, add the lime juice, ginger, almond butter, onion, water, garlic, agave, red pepper flakes, and sea salt. Process until smooth and creamy.

3. Pour the dressing over the vegetables and massage into the mixture with very clean hands for 2–3 minutes.

4. Cover and refrigerate the salad for an hour or two, allowing it to rest and absorb the flavors.

5. Garnish with the sunflower seeds before serving.

CREAMY POTATO SALAD

This is a traditional potato salad that has the perfect blend of celery, onions, and seasonings. This salad was popular during our Jumpstart program, and the recipe was highly requested.

2½ pounds red potatoes, unpeeled

4 celery stalks, thinly sliced

½ red onion, cut in half again and julienned

6 green onions, sliced

½ cup Tofu Cashew Mayonnaise (page 139)

4 teaspoons apple cider vinegar

2 tablespoons Dijon mustard

1 teaspoon agave nectar

½ teaspoon sea salt

¼ teaspoon black pepper

Yields: 6 servings
Prep Time: 20 minutes   *Cook Time:* 15 minutes

1. Cut the potatoes into ½- to 1-inch chunks.

2. Place the potatoes in a large pot and cover with water. Bring to a boil over medium-high heat; boil the potatoes for 5–10 minutes, then turn the heat down to medium. Cook until the potatoes are tender.

3. Rinse the potatoes in a colander with cold water until they are room temperature. Place the potatoes in a large mixing bowl.

4. Add the remaining ingredients to the potatoes and gently stir thoroughly.

DIXIE CAVIAR

This is an easy and delicious recipe that goes nicely as a side salad, a snack with baked tortilla chips, or served over a bed of greens to make a hearty salad.

Two 15-ounce cans black-eyed peas, drained and rinsed

2 cups corn (fresh or frozen)

2 tomatoes, finely chopped

1 green bell pepper, seeded and diced small

1 red bell pepper, seeded and diced small

1 red onion, diced small

4 green onions, sliced

2 jalapeño peppers, seeded and minced

3 garlic cloves, minced

¾ cup Italian Dressing (page 134)

¼ cup chopped fresh cilantro

½ cup Vegan Sour Cream (page 144) (optional)

Yields: 6 servings
Prep Time: 15 minutes   *Cook Time:* 0 minutes

1. Combine all the ingredients except the cilantro and sour cream and chill for 24 hours.

2. To serve, spoon the mixture into a serving bowl and stir in the cilantro. Top with the vegan sour cream.

GREEK SALAD

I love Greek salad but mainly because I love the flavor of feta cheese. This tofu feta is a great replacement and has the same tangy flavor of real feta cheese.

6–8 ounces extra-firm tofu

1 small red onion, thinly sliced

4 tablespoons red wine vinegar, divided

½ teaspoon agave nectar

1½ teaspoons lemon juice

½ teaspoon sea salt, plus more as needed

⅛ teaspoon black pepper, plus more as needed

1 teaspoon dried basil

1 teaspoon dried oregano

⅛ teaspoon dried rosemary

1 tablespoon nutritional yeast flakes

1 tablespoon chopped parsley

4 cups chopped romaine lettuce

2 cucumbers, diced

2 cups halved cherry tomatoes

1 cup kalamata olives

Yields: 4 servings
Prep Time: 25 minutes   *Cook Time:* 0 minutes

1. Drain the tofu and crumble. Set aside.

2. Place the onion, 2 tablespoons of the vinegar, and agave in a resealable plastic bag and let marinate in the refrigerator for 2 hours.

3. Mix the remaining 2 tablespoons vinegar, lemon juice, salt, pepper, basil, oregano, rosemary, nutritional yeast, and parsley in a small bowl. Add to the crumbled tofu, toss to combine, set aside, and let rest for 10 minutes.

4. Toss together the lettuce, cucumbers, tomatoes, and olives in a large bowl. Add the marinated onions and tofu feta cheese.

5. Toss gently and season with salt and pepper.

MARINATED TOMATO AND CUCUMBER SALAD

This is a delicious, fresh salad that is perfect when tomatoes, cucumbers, and basil are in season.

4 tomatoes, sliced and
    halved, or 1 pint cherry
    tomatoes, halved

1 cucumber, peeled and diced

1 small red onion, sliced

¼ cup chopped fresh basil

3 garlic cloves, minced

½ cup red wine vinegar

1 tablespoon agave nectar

½ teaspoon sea salt

¼ teaspoon black pepper

Yields: 4 servings
Prep Time: 15 minutes   *Cook Time:* 0 minutes

1. Place the vegetables in a mixing bowl.

2. Add the remaining ingredients, mixing gently, and let marinate in the refrigerator for 2–3 hours.

MEDITERRANEAN BARLEY

This salad of barley, chickpeas, arugula, and a beautiful mixture of vegetables in a balsamic vinegar sauce is a meal in itself.

1 cup pearl barley, uncooked

2 cups water

1 cup arugula leaves or mixed salad greens

1 red bell pepper, seeded and diced small

¼ cup chopped sun-dried tomatoes, rehydrated in hot water and then drained

½ cup small-diced red onion

One 15-ounce can chickpeas, rinsed and drained

1 cup chopped kalamata olives

2 tablespoons lemon juice

2 tablespoons balsamic vinegar

1 teaspoon sea salt

¼ teaspoon red pepper flakes

3 tablespoons pistachios, chopped

Yields: 4 servings
Prep Time: 15 minutes *Cook Time:* 35 minutes

1. In a pot, cook the barley in the water according to package directions. Remove from the heat and let cool.

2. Combine the cooked barley, arugula, bell pepper, sun-dried tomatoes, red onion, chickpeas, and olives in a mixing bowl.

3. Sprinkle with the lemon juice, balsamic vinegar, salt, and red pepper flakes and toss well.

4. Top with the pistachios and serve.

Quinoa Tabbouleh Salad

Tabbouleh is a Middle Eastern salad that is often made with bulgur wheat. This recipe uses quinoa instead of bulgur, which we love because quinoa is a tender, nutty grain packed full of nutrients. This tabbouleh includes a zesty blend of herbs, fresh vegetables, and seasonings.

1 cup red quinoa, uncooked

2 cups water or low-sodium vegetable stock

1 tablespoon smashed and chopped roasted garlic

1 tomato, diced

¼ cup lemon juice

1 teaspoon red wine vinegar

1 cucumber, diced medium

¼ teaspoon red pepper flakes

½ cup sliced green onions

¼ cup chopped fresh parsley

1 tablespoon chopped fresh mint

¼ teaspoon sea salt

⅛ teaspoon black pepper

Yields: 4 servings
Prep Time: 15 minutes   *Cook Time:* 15 minutes

1. Rinse the quinoa, which can have a bitter taste if not rinsed thoroughly. Add the quinoa and the water to a pot, bring to a boil over medium-high heat, then reduce the heat to a simmer. Cover and cook until all the liquid is absorbed.

2. Combine all ingredients, including cooked quinoa, in a mixing bowl, folding to blend well.

3. Store in an airtight container and allow to marinate for at least 1 hour to obtain optimum flavors. Serve chilled.

Southwestern Bean Salad

This recipe is for bean lovers. Seasoned perfectly to give it a Southwestern flavor, the beans, corn, and avocado also make this a satisfying salad that everyone will love.

One 15-ounce can pinto beans, drained and rinsed

One 15-ounce can black beans, drained and rinsed

1 cup frozen corn, thawed

1 red bell pepper, seeded and diced

½ cup diced medium red onion

1 cup halved or quartered cherry tomatoes

1 avocado, pitted and diced

¼ cup red wine vinegar

¼ cup lime juice

1 tablespoon agave nectar

½ teaspoon sea salt

½ teaspoon ground cumin

½ teaspoon chili powder

2 teaspoons Sriracha

¼ cup chopped fresh cilantro

Yields: 4–6 servings
Prep Time: 20 minutes   *Cook Time:* 0 minutes

1. Combine the beans and vegetables in a large bowl. Don't hesitate to add different vegetables depending on what is in season.

2. Blend the vinegar, lime juice, agave, salt, cumin, chili powder, and Sriracha in a small bowl. Add more chili powder and Sriracha if you like it spicier!

3. Drizzle over the beans and vegetables and toss to coat.

4. Refrigerate for an hour and then sprinkle with the cilantro before serving.

WARM SPINACH AND MUSHROOM SALAD

This salad can be a meal by itself or served as a side dish. It's the perfect combination of raw spinach wilted with hot mushrooms, onions, and seasonings.

10 ounces fresh baby spinach, washed and dried

6 tablespoons Balsamic Vinaigrette Dressing (page 124)

1 teaspoon Dijon mustard

½ cup low-sodium vegetable stock, for sautéing

6 ounces button mushrooms, sliced

½ red onion, sliced

3–4 cloves garlic, minced

¼ teaspoon sea salt

⅛ teaspoon black pepper

¼ cup slivered almonds, toasted

2 tablespoons vegan bacon bits

Yields: 4 servings
Prep Time: 10 minutes   *Cook Time:* 5–6 minutes

1. Preheat oven to 375°F.

2. In an oven-safe bowl or casserole dish, combine the spinach, balsamic vinaigrette, and Dijon.

3. Heat a sauté pan with a small amount of vegetable stock. Sauté small batches of sliced mushrooms, onion, and garlic until golden, 2–3 minutes.

4. Pour the warm mushrooms and onion into the bowl with the spinach and then toss to coat.

5. Place the bowl into the oven for 3 minutes, then remove and toss the salad again. Season with salt and pepper.

6. Garnish with the toasted almonds and vegan bacon bits.

THE 10-DAY JUMPSTART PROGRAM

THE JUMPSTART PROGRAM shown in *PlantPure Nation* is a 10-day program designed to allow participants to see and feel the benefits of a plant-based diet. Participants begin by getting a biometric test, including measurements of their weight and cholesterol levels, followed by an education session. Then, for the next 10 days, they are supplied with plant-based lunches and dinners prepared in a fresh production kitchen. On the eleventh day, participants are given the same biometric test so they can see how their numbers have changed.

Typically, the effects are dramatic. And more than 90 percent of the people who go through the program make the commitment to continue a plant-based diet.

Nelson Campbell addresses program participants during the first
Jumpstart session in Mebane, North Carolina

Sauces, Marinades, and Dressings

Balsamic BBQ Sauce

This sauce can be used for many dishes. I like to use it for BBQ Jackfruit (page 153) or for marinating vegetables.

1 cup balsamic vinegar

1 cup low-sodium ketchup (no high-fructose corn syrup)

½ cup apple cider vinegar

¼ cup maple syrup

1 tablespoon molasses

2 tablespoons whole-grain mustard

1½ teaspoons hot sauce

2 teaspoons vegan Worcestershire sauce

½ teaspoon sea salt

Yields: 1 cup
Prep Time: 5 minutes   *Cook Time:* 25 minutes

1. In a saucepan, cook the balsamic vinegar over medium heat until it reduces down by about a third.

2. Reduce heat to low, add the remaining ingredients, and cook for about 20 minutes, until thickened.

Balsamic Vinaigrette Dressing

Dates give this mild dressing the perfect sweetness, while the chia seeds help create a thick consistency.

½ cup balsamic vinegar

½ cup water

6 Medjool dates, pitted

1 garlic clove

2 teaspoons Italian Seasoning (page 147)

1 tablespoon lemon juice

2 teaspoons chia seeds

¼ teaspoon sea salt

Yields: 1¼ cups
Prep Time: 5 minutes   *Cook Time:* 0 minutes

1. Place all the ingredients in a Vitamix or other blender and blend thoroughly for 20 seconds.

2. Store in the refrigerator.

> **KIM'S HINTS:** Chia seeds act as a thickener in this recipe and they add important nutrients. However, if you don't have any available, you can also use a pinch (⅛ teaspoon) of xanthan gum to thicken the dressing. Xanthan gum gets thick and gummy very quickly, so use only a pinch.

BLUE CHEEZ DRESSING

This is a crowd-pleaser. It is very rich, so you don't need much! I serve this with Cauliflower Buffalo Bites (page 77), Buffalo Tofu Hoagie (page 154), and Buffalo Beans and Greens (page 185). This dressing is also a great addition to any salad or burger.

½ cup Tofu Cashew
  Mayonnaise (page 139)

1 garlic clove

½ teaspoon agave nectar

2 tablespoons lemon juice

2 teaspoons white miso paste

2 teaspoons apple cider
  vinegar

2 tablespoons tahini

¼ teaspoon sea salt

2 tablespoons finely chopped
  green onions or parsley

¼ cup crumbled extra-firm
  tofu

Yields: 1 cup or 4–6 servings
Prep Time: 10 minutes   *Cook Time:* 0 minutes

1. Place the mayonnaise, garlic, agave, lemon juice, miso, vinegar, tahini, and salt into a Vitamix or other blender and blend until smooth and creamy.

2. Pour dressing into a bowl, then add the green onions and crumbled tofu, stirring gently with a spoon.

3. If you prefer a thinner dressing, simply add nondairy milk or water.

CAESAR DRESSING

This creamy dressing is delicious on any salad. A typical Caesar dressing calls for anchovies, which impart a unique flavor. However, I use seaweed, which adds a similar fish taste. This recipe requires a batch of Tofu Cashew Mayonnaise (page 139).

½ cup Tofu Cashew
Mayonnaise (page 139)

1 teaspoon Dijon mustard

¾ teaspoon low-sodium
soy sauce

½ teaspoon nutritional yeast
flakes

1¾ teaspoons smashed and
chopped roasted garlic

½ teaspoon dried, finely
chopped wakame seaweed
or any type of sea
seasoning blend

½ cup low-sodium vegetable
stock

Yields: 6
Prep Time: 5 minutes   *Cook Time:* 0 minutes

1. Place all the ingredients in a Vitamix or other blender and process until smooth.

KIM'S HINTS: If you do not have dried wakame, I have used part of a nori sheet ripped into small pieces. Serve this dressing with mixed greens and fat-free croutons.

CASHEW CREAM

This recipe is for a creamy, cashew-based milk that can be used in various dishes as a thickener and overall flavor enhancer. When traditional recipes call for heavy cream or a soy creamer, I like to use cashew cream. Use this cream sparingly, though, as it is a high-fat plant food.

1 cup raw cashews, soaked in water to cover for 2–3 hours, then drained

2 cups water

Yields: 8 servings
Prep Time: 5 minutes   *Cook Time:* 0 minutes

1. Soaking the cashews in water for a few hours will reduce blending time. If you are not using a Vitamix, I highly recommend soaking the cashews so they blend into a smooth and creamy texture.

2. Place the cashews and 2 cups fresh water (do not use the soaking water) in a Vitamix or other high-powered blender. Blend on high until smooth and creamy.

3. Store in the refrigerator for up to a week.

CAULIFLOWER ALFREDO SAUCE

Our cashew-based Fettuccine Alfredo (page 197) is always a hit, but if you want a lighter version, this is a great alternative. This sauce is excellent over pastas, steamed veggies, or baked potatoes; as a dip for tortilla chips; or as a spread for sandwiches.

1 cauliflower head, broken into florets

½ teaspoon garlic powder

1 teaspoon onion powder

2 cups nondairy milk

¼ cup nutritional yeast flakes

1 tablespoon Dijon mustard

½ teaspoon sea salt

½ teaspoon black pepper

Yields: 4–6 servings
Prep Time: 10 minutes   *Cook Time:* 15 minutes

1. Bring a large pot of water to a boil and add the cauliflower florets. Boil for about 15 minutes, or until tender.

2. Strain the cauliflower and add to a Vitamix or other blender with the remaining ingredients. Add more or less nondairy milk for a thinner or thicker consistency. Blend until smooth and creamy.

CILANTRO-WASABI AIOLI

I like to think of aioli as a flavored mayonnaise. This aioli is a special combination of wasabi, cilantro, cashews, and tofu. A green delight!

¼ cup raw cashews, soaked in water to cover for 2–3 hours, then drained

¼ cup water

¼ cup silken tofu

1 clove garlic

1 teaspoon wasabi paste

1 teaspoon low-sodium soy sauce

½ teaspoon lemon juice

1 teaspoon pureed ginger

1 tablespoon apple cider vinegar

1 tablespoon chopped fresh cilantro

½ teaspoon sea salt

Yields: 8 servings
Prep Time: 10 minutes   *Cook Time:* 0 minutes

1. Soaking the cashews in water for a few hours will reduce blending time. If you are not using a Vitamix, I highly recommend soaking the cashews so they blend into a smooth and creamy texture.

2. Combine all the ingredients in a Vitamix or other high-powered blender and process on high speed until smooth and creamy.

3. Remove from the blender and chill to thicken. Serve chilled.

CREAMY CHIPOTLE AND BLACK PEPPERCORN DRESSING 🌱

This dressing requires that you have a batch of Tofu Cashew Mayonnaise (page 139) on hand. It's a great topping for Easy Black Bean Burgers (page 157). I also use this recipe in a variation of my Creamy Potato Salad (page 109) to give it a unique flavor.

¾ teaspoon lemon juice

1¼ cups Tofu Cashew Mayonnaise (page 139)

1½ teaspoons apple cider vinegar

1¾ teaspoons Dijon mustard

½ teaspoon low-sodium soy sauce

1 teaspoon onion powder

¾ teaspoon chipotle chili powder

1 tablespoon nutritional yeast flakes

2 tablespoons low-sodium vegetable stock

1 teaspoon black peppercorns

Yields: 6–8 servings
Prep Time: 10 minutes   *Cook Time:* 0 minutes

1. Combine all the ingredients in a blender and blend until smooth.

2. Remove from the blender and chill in an airtight container in the refrigerator for at least 1 hour before using.

KIM'S HINTS: This dressing can have too much heat for some people. I recommend you add the chipotle chili powder in ¼-teaspoon increments, taste, and add more if desired. About ¾ teaspoon is perfect for me, but I like some heat.

HERB CASHEW SALAD DRESSING

Here's a plant-based dressing that is better than ranch! The secret: cashews, herbs, and seasonings.

¼ cup raw cashews, soaked in water to cover for 2–3 hours, then drained

½ cup water

¼ cup chopped fresh parsley

½ teaspoon sea salt

1 teaspoon tahini

1 tablespoon white miso paste

¼ teaspoon black pepper

1 tablespoon lemon juice

½ cup silken tofu

¼ cup apple cider vinegar

Yields: 6 servings
Prep Time: 5–10 minutes   *Cook Time:* 0 minutes

1. Soaking the cashews in water for a few hours will reduce blending time. If you are not using a Vitamix, I highly recommend soaking the cashews so they blend into a smooth and creamy texture.

2. Place all ingredients in a Vitamix or other high-powered blender and process on high speed until smooth and creamy.

3. Remove from the blender and chill for 1 hour before using.

KIM'S HINT: Silken tofu is not always available in the supermarkets, so you can also use a firm tofu and add a little more water. Silken tofu is simply watered-down tofu.

ITALIAN DRESSING

This easy and quick Italian dressing is oil free and full of flavor.

1 cup low-sodium vegetable
  stock

¼ cup red wine vinegar

1 tablespoon Dijon mustard

1½ teaspoons agave nectar

3 garlic cloves, minced

1 teaspoon Italian Seasoning
  (page 147)

¼ teaspoon sea salt

¼ teaspoon black pepper

⅛ teaspoon paprika

⅛ teaspoon xanthan gum,
  plus more as needed

Yields: 6 servings
Prep Time: 10 minutes   *Cook Time:* 0 minutes

1. Place all the ingredients in a blender and blend on high speed for 5–10 seconds.

2. Add more xanthan gum slowly if you like your dressing thicker. Be careful with xanthan gum; it only requires a pinch to thicken the dressing.

KIM'S HINT: If you don't have xanthan gum on hand, you also can use ½–1 teaspoon of chia seeds to thicken the dressing.

Marinara Sauce

This marinara sauce goes great on pizza, spaghetti, lasagna, or anything Italian. Make it in large batches and freeze it so you never have to buy another jar of marinara sauce!

6 garlic cloves, minced

1 onion, diced

3 carrots, diced small

¼ cup low-sodium vegetable stock, for sautéing

1 cup fresh basil, chopped

3 tablespoons tomato paste

1 tablespoon dried oregano

¼ teaspoon red pepper flakes

½ teaspoon sea salt

¼ teaspoon black pepper

Two 14-ounce cans crushed tomatoes

1 cup water

1 tablespoon agave nectar

¼ cup dry red wine

Yields: 6 servings

Prep Time: 15 minutes   *Cook Time:* 80 minutes

1. In a large pot over medium-high heat, sauté the garlic, onion, and carrots in the vegetable stock until tender.

2. Add the basil, tomato paste, oregano, red pepper flakes, salt, and pepper. Cook over low heat for 5 minutes.

3. Pour in the crushed tomatoes, water, agave, and wine.

4. Bring to a boil, then lower the heat to a simmer. Simmer for 1 hour, uncovered, stirring occasionally.

RUSSIAN DRESSING

This dressing is the perfect flavor combination of tomatoes, pickles, and mustard. It goes well on any sandwich or veggie burger.

¼ cup Tofu Cashew Mayonnaise (page 139)

4 teaspoons low-sodium ketchup (no high-fructose corn syrup)

2 teaspoons chopped sweet or dill pickle or pickle relish

1 teaspoon Dijon mustard

Yields: 4 servings
Prep Time: 10 minutes   *Cook Time:* 0 minutes

1. Mix all the ingredients together in a small bowl until well combined.

SWEET TAHINI DRESSING

This mild tahini dressing has a hint of maple syrup and balsamic vinegar.

¼ cup tahini

¼ cup water

1 tablespoon maple syrup

¼ cup balsamic vinegar

3 tablespoons lemon juice

2 garlic cloves, minced

2 tablespoons chopped fresh
  parsley

1 teaspoon white miso paste

½ teaspoon sea salt

Yields: 4–6 servings
Prep Time: 10 minutes   *Cook Time:* 0 minutes

1. Place all the ingredients in a blender and process until smooth.

TOFU CASHEW MAYONNAISE

This plant-based mayonnaise is so rich and full of flavor that you will not miss your old egg- and oil-based mayonnaise. This entire recipe only uses ¼ cup of raw cashews, which makes it lower in fat than other commercially prepared vegan mayonnaises. I like to make a batch every week or two to have on hand—consider it part of your pantry! I use this mayonnaise for sandwiches, dressings, and sauces.

¼ cup raw cashews, soaked in water to cover for 2–3 hours, then drained

7 ounces extra-firm tofu

½ teaspoon sea salt

½ teaspoon tahini

4 teaspoons lemon juice

1½ teaspoons white vinegar

1 tablespoon Dijon mustard

2 tablespoons apple cider vinegar

2½ teaspoons agave nectar

2 tablespoons water

¼ teaspoon xanthan gum

Yields: 2 cups
Prep Time: 10 minutes   *Cook Time:* 0 minutes

1. Soaking the cashews in water for a few hours will reduce blending time. If you are not using a Vitamix, I highly recommend soaking the cashews so they blend into a smooth and creamy texture.

2. Place all the ingredients in a Vitamix or other high-powered blender. Blend until smooth and shiny.

KIM'S HINT: If you do not have xanthan gum available you can skip this ingredient but the mayonnaise might have a slightly thinner consistency.

Tzatziki Sauce

This is a creamy Greek sauce that is mayonnaise-based. It has a slightly tangy flavor with a fresh taste of cucumbers and dill. This sauce goes perfectly on top of our popular Zucchini Cakes (page 242). You also can use this sauce as a creamy salad dressing.

¾ cup Tofu Cashew Mayonnaise (page 139)

2 teaspoons lemon juice

4 teaspoons water

½ cucumber, peeled and finely diced

2 tablespoons finely diced red onion

1 teaspoon dried dill weed

Yields: 4 servings
Prep Time: 10 minutes   *Cook Time:* 0 minutes

1. Mix all the ingredients thoroughly.

VEGAN MUSHROOM GRAVY

This rich, flavorful gravy is perfect over potatoes and Beanie Veggie Loaf (page 178). It's easy to prepare and inexpensive.

1 onion, minced

6 white button mushrooms, chopped

2½ cups low-sodium vegetable stock, divided

½ teaspoon minced garlic

½ teaspoon dried thyme

½ teaspoon dried sage

½ teaspoon crushed dried rosemary

1 tablespoon cooking sherry

2 tablespoons tamari sauce or low-sodium soy sauce

1 tablespoon nutritional yeast flakes

¼ cup flour

⅛ teaspoon sea salt

¼ teaspoon black pepper

Yields: 4 servings
Prep Time: 10 minutes   *Cook Time:* 10–15 minutes

1. In a large skillet over medium-high heat, sauté the onion and mushrooms in ½ cup of the vegetable stock.

2. Add the garlic, thyme, sage, rosemary, sherry, tamari, and nutritional yeast, then continue to sauté for just a minute or two over high heat.

3. Pour the remaining vegetable stock into a bowl and whisk in the flour until there are no lumps. Add to the pan with the onion and mushrooms. Simmer over medium heat, stirring, until the gravy has reached its peak thickness, about 10 minutes. Add salt and pepper to taste.

Vegan Sour Cream

A delightfully cool and creamy addition that complements most Mexican or spicy dishes, this sour cream has more flavor than any store-bought version.

½ cup raw cashews, soaked in water to cover for 2–3 hours, then drained

¼ cup water

1 cup silken tofu

3 tablespoons lemon juice

1 teaspoon agave nectar

1 teaspoon white miso paste

¼ teaspoon sea salt

Yields: 6 servings
Prep Time: 5–10 minutes   *Cook Time:* 0 minutes

1. Soaking the cashews in water for a few hours will reduce blending time. If you are not using a Vitamix, I highly recommend soaking the cashews so they blend into a smooth and creamy texture.

2. Combine all the ingredients in a Vitamix or other high-powered blender and blend until smooth and creamy.

3. Allow the mixture to chill for 1 hour to become thick.

Spices and Toppings

BERBERE SPICE

This is a combination spice used in many Ethiopian recipes. Depending on where you buy this, you can get varied levels of heat. It's not always an easy spice to find, so I did once purchase some online. However, I discovered that simply making my own is cheaper and more adaptable. Here's a mild-heat version.

2 teaspoons ground cumin

1 teaspoon ground cardamom

½ teaspoon ground allspice

1 teaspoon ground fenugreek

1 teaspoon ground coriander

¼ teaspoon ground cloves

1 teaspoon black pepper

4 teaspoons red pepper flakes

1 teaspoon ground ginger

1 teaspoon ground turmeric

3 tablespoons paprika

½ teaspoon ground cinnamon

Yields: 6–7 tablespoons
Prep Time: 5–10 minutes   *Cook Time:* 0 minutes

1. Mix all the ingredients and store in an airtight container in a cool, dry place.

GARAM MASALA

This spice blend, a combination of eight different spices, is used in many Indian dishes.

1 tablespoon ground cumin

1½ teaspoons ground coriander

1½ teaspoons ground cardamom

1½ teaspoons black pepper

1 teaspoon ground cinnamon

½ teaspoon ground cloves

½ teaspoon ground nutmeg

1 teaspoon ground ginger

Yields: 3 tablespoons
Prep Time: 5–10 minutes   *Cook Time:* 0 minutes

1. Mix all the ingredients and store in an airtight container in a cool, dry place.

Italian Seasoning

This is my favorite blend of Italian seasonings. It's great in marinara sauces, pizzas, and salad dressings. Try sprinkling some on fresh tomatoes and garden vegetables.

1 tablespoon dried oregano
1 tablespoon dried basil
1 tablespoon dried rosemary
1 tablespoon dried thyme
1 tablespoon dried marjoram

Yields: 5 tablespoons
Prep Time: 5 minutes   *Cook Time:* 0 minutes

1. Mix all the ingredients and store in an airtight container in a cool, dry place.

Mexican Spice Blend

It's much easier to have these types of blends handy instead of pulling spices out and trying to play with their flavors. We love this blend and use it for many dishes.

2 tablespoons ground cumin
4 tablespoons chili powder
2 tablespoons smoked
   paprika
1 teaspoon dried oregano
1 tablespoon garlic powder
¼ teaspoon cayenne pepper
¼ teaspoon red pepper flakes
1 teaspoon onion powder
1 tablespoon black pepper

Yields: 10–11 tablespoons
Prep Time: 5–10 minutes   *Cook Time:* 0 minutes

1. Mix all the ingredients and store in an airtight container in a cool, dark place.

Pumpkin Pie Spice

Use this spice blend in pumpkin pie, cakes, cookies, pancakes, and oatmeal.

4 tablespoons ground
  cinnamon
4 teaspoons ground nutmeg
4 teaspoons ground ginger
1 tablespoon ground allspice

Yields: scant ½ cup
Prep Time: 5 minutes   *Cook Time:* 0 minutes

1. Mix all the ingredients and store in an airtight container in a cool, dry place.

Vegan Parmesan Sprinkle

This rich topping helps bring out a cheesy Italian flavor. I like to put it on spaghetti, pesto pasta, and pizza.

⅓ cup nutritional yeast flakes
¼ cup blanched raw almond
  slivers
¾ cup raw cashews
½ teaspoon sea salt
¼ teaspoon garlic powder

Yields: 1 cup
Prep Time: 5–10 minutes   *Cook Time:* 0 minutes

1. Place all the ingredients in a food processor and grind into a powder. Store in an airtight container in the fridge.

THE MEBANE EXPERIMENT

MEBANE IS A SMALL, rural town in North Carolina with a population just over 12,000. The town traces its beginnings to the early nineteenth century when a post office was established in 1809. The town was named for Brigadier General Alexander Mebane of the North Carolina Militia, who was also a member of Congress in the 1790s. In 1855, the railroad arrived, and Mebane was incorporated in 1881 as the town of Mebanesville. The name was officially changed to Mebane in 1883. In 1881, Mebane's industrial growth began with the establishment of the White Furniture Company, which finally closed its doors for good in 1993 after more than 100 years in business. The economy today is more diversified, and includes companies that make bedsprings and mattresses, fire detection and suppression equipment, and cash-handling machines.

Downtown Mebane, North Carolina

The Mebane experiment in *PlantPure Nation* was conceived by Nelson Campbell to prove that a plant-based diet could be widely appealing to mainstream consumers—even those steeped in the South's tradition of rich "comfort food." Many of the people who live in Mebane don't belong to the demographic that's often targeted by professional marketing consultants in the wellness business. But Nelson strongly believes that people everywhere—regardless of their socioeconomic status—care about their own and their families' health.

The experiment was wildly successful. After participating in Nelson's 10-day Jumpstart program (see "The 10-Day Jumpstart Program" on page 122), the vast majority of Jumpstarters saw significant drops in their total cholesterol, LDL cholesterol, and triglyceride levels, and many shed pounds without any additional exercise. The average total cholesterol generally fell 20 to 25 percent. For example, if a group started out at 200 mg/dL, the average participant's cholesterol would fall to 150 or so. One person's cholesterol went down 134 points in 10 days, and two people saw their LDL cholesterol (the "bad" cholesterol) fall by about half. Perhaps most amazing, many people who were on cholesterol-lowering and other medications had the option of getting off those medications at the end of the Jumpstart.

The word spread fast. In only five months, Nelson went from a group of 16 to a group of 130, with many people having to be turned away due to logistical constraints. And in post-Jumpstart questionnaires, more than 90 *percent* of participants expressed their desire to continue a plant-based lifestyle. Nelson and his team had irrefutably proved his point: a plant-based diet could indeed be embraced in a mainstream community like Mebane, North Carolina.

Sandwiches, Burgers, and Wraps

Avocado—White Bean Salad Wrap

This recipe has the perfect combination of beans, avocados, spinach, and carrots. The orange juice and seasonings give this filling a fresh, slightly sweet flavor.

1 avocado, pitted and peeled

One 15-ounce can cannellini beans, rinsed and drained

½ cup small-diced red bell pepper

1 small red onion, diced medium

1 carrot, shredded

1 cup thinly sliced spinach

2 tablespoons nutritional yeast flakes

1 tablespoon sunflower seeds (raw or roasted)

1–2 teaspoons Sriracha

¼ teaspoon sea salt

¼ teaspoon black pepper

2 tablespoons lemon juice

1 tablespoon orange juice

1 teaspoon apple cider vinegar

4 large whole-grain tortillas

2 cups sprouts or shredded lettuce

Yields: 4 wraps
Prep Time: 15 minutes   *Cook Time:* 0 minutes

1. In a medium-size mixing bowl, mash the avocados and beans until creamy with some chunks still remaining.

2. Fold the bell pepper, onion, carrot, and spinach into the avocado mixture.

3. Add the nutritional yeast flakes, sunflower seeds, Sriracha, salt, and pepper; fold to combine.

4. Mix the citrus juices and vinegar in a small cup. Fold this liquid into the avocado–white bean mixture. Continue folding until well combined and the veggies begin to soak into the creamy liquid.

5. Divide the mixture among the whole-grain tortillas, cover each filling with ½ cup sprouts, and wrap.

KIM'S HINT: I like to add even more Sriracha to our wraps for extra heat.

BBQ Jackfruit

Green jackfruit is often referred to as the vegetarian's meat. It is the fruit of a tree native to South Asia and Southeast Asia. When green jackfruit cooks and softens, it begins to pull apart, taking on an appearance similar to pulled pork. The hardest part of this recipe is finding canned green jackfruit (available in most Asian markets). You can occasionally find fresh green jackfruit, but it's extremely messy, sticky, and difficult to cut.

Two 20-ounce cans green jackfruit in water, drained

1½ cups barbecue sauce

1 onion, diced

1 green bell pepper, seeded and diced medium

Kim's Hints:

- Make this recipe your own with whatever barbecue sauce you decide to use. It's really up to you, since there are so many barbecue flavors available. Be sure to choose sauces with no added oils and a low sodium content.
- This recipe gets better the longer you cook it. The jackfruit falls apart like tender pulled pork and absorbs flavor perfectly. In fact, we like it better as leftovers!
- Serve this recipe on a whole wheat bun and top with coleslaw. This goes perfectly with baked sweet potato fries!

Yields: 4–6 servings
Prep Time: 5 minutes   *Cook Time:* 5–7 hours

1. Rinse the green jackfruit thoroughly.

2. Place all the ingredients in a slow cooker and cook on medium heat for 4–5 hours. Jackfruit will begin to fall apart and have the consistency of pulled pork.

3. After cooking for 4–5 hours, use a fork to pull apart the fruit and stir thoroughly.

4. Turn the slow cooker to low heat and cook for another 1–2 hours.

BUFFALO TOFU HOAGIE 🌱

Nelson and my son, Colin, love buffalo sauce. I also grew up in western New York near the home of the original buffalo wing sauce recipe, so I included three buffalo-style recipes in this cookbook. Just be careful to choose a buffalo sauce for these recipes with no added oils. This sandwich is made from marinated tofu layered with mushrooms, onions, and peppers on a whole wheat hoagie roll. Serve it with our vegan Blue Cheez Dressing and you will have a hit.

One 14-ounce block extra-firm tofu

1 cup oil-free buffalo wing sauce

1 onion, sliced into half rings

8 ounces mushrooms, sliced

1 red or green bell pepper, seeded and sliced

¼ cup low-sodium vegetable stock, for sautéing

Sea salt to taste

Black pepper to taste

1 tomato, sliced

6 whole wheat hoagie rolls, toasted

2 cups fresh sprouts

Blue Cheez Dressing (page 125)

Celery sticks, for serving

Yields: 6 hoagies
Prep Time: 10 minutes   *Cook Time:* 20 minutes

1. Preheat oven to 375°F. Line a baking sheet with parchment paper and set aside.

2. Drain the tofu and gently press between layers of paper towels to remove excess moisture. Another trick is to freeze and thaw the tofu, causing it to firm up with a sponge-like consistency.

3. Slice the tofu into thin triangles. You should be able to get 16 triangles from one 14-ounce tofu block. I like the look of triangles, but you can choose any cut.

4. Coat the tofu with the buffalo sauce. Save any extra sauce and use it on your hoagie when assembling.

5. Place the tofu on the prepared baking sheet and bake for 10–20 minutes until edges are browned and dried, turning halfway through.

6. In a skillet over medium-high heat, sauté the onion, mushrooms, and bell pepper in the vegetable stock and season with salt and pepper. Cook the vegetables until tender.

7. Place the sliced tomatoes on the toasted hoagie rolls.

8. Layer with the baked tofu triangles, vegetables, sprouts, and any extra buffalo sauce.

9. Serve with the Blue Cheez Dressing and celery sticks.

EASY BLACK BEAN BURGER

This veggie burger is both easy and quick. I like to make a large batch and freeze the leftovers. They are hearty and wholesome.

Two 15-ounce cans black beans, rinsed and drained

1 tablespoon flax meal

3 tablespoons hot water

¾ cup dry oats

½ cup cooked brown rice

½ cup minced onion

¾ cup corn (fresh or frozen)

1 teaspoon ground cumin

½ teaspoon sea salt

1 teaspoon Mrs. Dash Southwest Chipotle Seasoning Blend or Mexican Spice Blend (page 147)

3 tablespoons diced tomato or salsa

Yields: 6–8 burgers
Prep Time: 10 minutes   *Cook Time:* 20–30 minutes

1. Preheat oven to 375°F. Line a baking sheet with parchment paper and set aside.

2. Mash the beans coarsely with a fork or potato masher in a mixing bowl. You don't want to puree the beans, so leave some half chunks remaining.

3. In a small bowl, soak the flax meal in the water and let sit for 2–3 minutes.

4. Add the flax meal mixture and the remaining ingredients to the mashed beans. Mix everything together with a fork until you have a uniform consistency. This will take a minute or two.

5. Form the bean mixture into the burger sizes that you like. It's helpful to have wet hands when forming the patties. You should get 6–8 burgers.

6. Place the patties on the prepared baking sheet and bake for 20–30 minutes, or until browned.

EDAMAME BURGER

Fresh edamame and Asian vegetables are used to create a delicious green burger served with a zesty Cilantro-Wasabi Aioli. These unique and popular burgers are wholesome and easy to prepare, and they always get rave reviews.

4 cups frozen shelled edamame, cooked

2 cups frozen mixed vegetable stir-fry blend, thawed

1 tablespoon flax meal

2 tablespoons hot water

¼ cup orange juice

¼ teaspoon low-sodium soy sauce

1 tablespoon agave nectar

¼ teaspoon Dijon mustard

1 cup whole wheat bread crumbs

½ teaspoon sea salt

¼ teaspoon black pepper

1 teaspoon lemon juice

6 whole wheat burger buns

6 green-leaf lettuce leaves

1½ cups sprouts

¾ cup Cilantro-Wasabi Aioli (page 131)

Yields: 6 burgers
Prep Time: 30 minutes   *Cook Time:* 30 minutes

1. Preheat oven to 375°F. Line a baking sheet with parchment paper and set aside.

2. Place the cooked edamame and thawed stir-fry blend into a food processor. Pulse multiple times until the ingredients are well blended. It should be green and have a fine consistency similar to that of short-grain rice.

3. In a small bowl, combine the flax meal and water. Allow to sit for 2–3 minutes.

4. Remove the vegetable mixture from the food processor and place in a large mixing bowl. Add the flax mixture and fold together.

5. Add the orange juice, soy sauce, agave, Dijon, bread crumbs, salt, pepper, and lemon juice to the vegetables and mix well.

6. Form into 6 patties and place on the prepared baking sheet.

7. Bake for 10–15 minutes. Flip and continue baking for an additional 10–15 minutes. Remove from the oven and allow the burgers to set for about 5 minutes before serving.

8. Serve on a whole wheat bun topped with lettuce, sprouts, and Cilantro-Wasabi Aioli.

> **KIM'S HINT:** You can use any combination of frozen Asian vegetable stir-fry blend that you have available. Be careful to select one that has no added oils or salts (do not use seasoned veggie blends, for example).

Eggless Tofu Salad

This tofu salad is an interesting spin on traditional egg salad. I love the fennel and curry powder because it gives the dish a unique flavor. This recipe is also versatile because you can add your favorite vegetables to it.

One 14-ounce block extra-firm tofu, drained and crumbled

¼ cup sliced green onion

⅓ cup finely chopped fennel

¼ cup Tofu Cashew Mayonnaise (page 139)

1 tablespoon Dijon mustard

2 tablespoons lemon juice

2 tablespoons chopped fresh parsley

1 teaspoon curry powder

2 teaspoons dried dill weed

¼ teaspoon paprika

¼ teaspoon ground cumin

¼ teaspoon sea salt

¼ teaspoon black pepper

Yields: 6 servings
Prep Time: 15 minutes   *Cook Time:* 0 minutes

1. Add the crumbled tofu to a large bowl.

2. Add the remaining ingredients and stir until the mixture is well combined.

3. Serve in a sandwich, in a wrap, or as a salad topping.

FRENCH DIP SANDWICH

This was a favorite traditional recipe that my mother prepared on special occasions. I converted it into a plant-based sandwich and it's amazing. I use mushrooms to replace the beef and a vegan horseradish aioli.

Horseradish Aioli

1 cup Tofu Cashew Mayonnaise (page 139)

2 garlic cloves, minced

1 teaspoon apple cider vinegar

1 teaspoon vegan Worcestershire sauce

4 green onions, sliced

2 tablespoons prepared horseradish

Au Jus Dipping Sauce

2 cups low-sodium mushroom stock

1 tablespoon cornstarch

1 tablespoon balsamic vinegar

1 tablespoon vegan Worcestershire sauce

Sea salt to taste

Black pepper to taste

1 onion, sliced into half rings

4 large portobello mushrooms, sliced

Sea salt to taste

Black pepper to taste

4 whole wheat sub rolls

Yields: 4 sandwiches
Prep Time: 15 minutes   *Cook Time:* 10–15 minutes

1. To make the horseradish aioli, blend the mayonnaise, garlic, vinegar, Worcestershire sauce, green onions, and horseradish using a food processor or mixing by hand in a bowl. Set aside.

2. To make the au jus dipping sauce, whisk together the mushroom stock, cornstarch, balsamic vinegar, and Worcestershire sauce in a saucepan over medium heat. Once the cornstarch is absorbed, turn the heat to medium-high. Cook, stirring, until thickened. Season with salt and pepper to taste. Set aside.

3. In a nonstick frying pan, sauté onion and mushrooms in ¼ cup of the au jus dipping sauce. Season with salt and pepper to taste.

4. Toast the sub rolls and spread the horseradish aioli generously on each bun, then cover with the mushroom mixture. Serve these subs warm with the dipping sauce on the side.

No-Tuna Tempeh Salad

If you miss tuna sandwiches, this might be the answer. Tempeh is the core ingredient, followed by onions, celery, and parsley. Using nori gives this filling a nice sea flavor.

4 ounces tempeh, crumbled

1 celery stalk, finely diced

3 green onions, sliced

2 tablespoons chopped fresh parsley

¼ teaspoon onion powder

¼ teaspoon garlic powder

½ sushi nori sheet, torn into small pieces

1½ teaspoons nutritional yeast flakes

¼ teaspoon paprika

¼ teaspoon sea salt

⅛ teaspoon black pepper

1 teaspoon vegan Worcestershire sauce

¼ cup Tofu Cashew Mayonnaise (page 139)

Yields: 4 servings
Prep Time: 20 minutes   *Cook Time:* 0 minutes

1. In a large bowl, stir together all the ingredients except the Tofu Cashew Mayonnaise. Mix thoroughly.

2. Add the mayonnaise and season with additional salt and pepper if desired.

3. Refrigerate until serving.

Kim's Hints:

- Eat this salad in a sandwich, as a grilled sandwich, on top of salad greens, or tossed with cooked pasta.
- If tempeh isn't your thing, try a can of coarsely chopped or mashed chickpeas.
- Feel free to add more vegetables to the filling.

REUBEN SANDWICH

My mother made the best Reuben sandwiches, with plenty of sauerkraut, corned beef, and Swiss cheese. These flavors bring back fond memories of my childhood in upstate New York. I was never a fan of the corned beef, so making a vegan version was easy: I simply replaced the meat with spinach, mushrooms, and tempeh. It's the sauerkraut and dressing that make this a unique sandwich.

6 ounces Lightlife Organic Smoky Tempeh Strips

⅓ cup Russian Dressing (page 137)

1 cup sauerkraut

1 red onion, thinly sliced

½ red bell pepper, seeded and sliced

6 ounces white button mushrooms, sliced

2 cups fresh spinach

1 teaspoon black pepper

8 slices rye bread

Yields: 4 sandwiches
Prep Time: 15 minutes   Cook Time: 25–30 minutes

1. Preheat oven to 425°F. Line a baking sheet with parchment paper.

2. Lay out the smoky tempeh strips on the prepared baking sheet and bake for 10–15 minutes or until edges become dry to the touch.

3. In a small mixing bowl, combine the Russian dressing and sauerkraut.

4. Using a very small amount of water, sauté the onion, bell pepper, and mushrooms in a skillet over medium-high heat until the mushrooms are softened. Add the spinach and heat until wilted. Season this mixture with black pepper.

5. Cover 4 slices of the bread with smoky tempeh strips and then top with the spinach mixture. On the remaining 4 slices, smear the Russian dressing mixture and place on top of the sandwiches.

6. Grill in a nonstick panini press or griddle until the desired grill marks are formed.

SLOPPY JOES

The bulk of this sandwich is wheat bulgur. It gives the filling a meaty texture and absorbs flavor perfectly. I prefer to use wheat bulgur instead of veggie meat products or textured vegetable protein because those products are highly processed and made from isolated soy protein, which is not a healthy whole food.

1¾ cups water, divided

¾ cup wheat bulgur, uncooked

1 onion, diced

6 ounces mushrooms, chopped

1 green bell pepper, seeded and diced medium

1 poblano pepper, seeded and diced small

4 garlic cloves, minced

1 celery stalk, finely diced

1 carrot, diced

1 tablespoon molasses

½ cup low-sodium ketchup (no high-fructose corn syrup)

2 tablespoons prepared yellow mustard

2 tablespoons vegan Worcestershire sauce

1 teaspoon chili powder

½ teaspoon sea salt

¼ teaspoon black pepper

4 whole wheat burger buns

Yields: 4 servings
Prep Time: 15 minutes   *Cook Time:* 20 minutes

1. Bring 1½ cups of the water to a boil in a saucepan over medium-high heat. Remove from the heat and stir in the bulgur wheat. Cover and let stand for 20 minutes. Drain any excess liquid.

2. In a skillet over medium-high heat, sauté all the vegetables in the remaining ¼ cup water. When the veggies are tender, add the molasses, ketchup, mustard, Worcestershire sauce, chili powder, salt, pepper, and cooked bulgur wheat and cook over low heat for 15 minutes. Stir often.

3. Serve on the whole wheat burger buns.

> **KIM'S HINT:** If you want to use more bulgur wheat, just keep the ratio of 2 parts water to 1 part bulgur wheat.

Stuffed Bagels

I originally learned about this recipe while watching a Rachael Ray show. I have always enjoyed her recipes because they are simple and quick comfort foods. My challenge is to veganize her recipes. The original stuffed bagel recipe is full of cheese, eggs, and oil. It wasn't too hard to convert it into a plant-based recipe. These remind me of a calzone—only bagel style. They are a bit time-consuming and labor-intensive, but they are great to have on hand for lunches, snacks, or on-the-go meals.

1 cup diced onion

6 ounces mushrooms, sliced

2 cups fresh spinach

2 tablespoons water

¼ teaspoon sea salt

¼ teaspoon black pepper

1 recipe Vegan Ricotta Cheese (page 99)

Naan Bread dough (page 67), unbaked

¼ cup sesame seeds

Yields: 8 bagels
Prep Time: 45 minutes
Cook Time: 60 minutes (includes rising)

1. Preheat oven to 375°F. Line a baking sheet with parchment paper and set aside.

2. In a skillet over medium-high heat, sauté the onion, mushrooms, and spinach in the water until tender and spinach is wilted. Season with salt and pepper. Drain thoroughly to remove the excess moisture.

3. In a bowl, fold the vegetables into the vegan ricotta cheese.

4. Divide the naan dough into 8 pieces. Place on a dry tray and allow to double in size, 30 minutes. Roll each piece into a rectangle about 4 × 6 inches.

5. Bring a very large pot of water to a boil over high heat. You will be dropping the bagels into this water, so make sure it is big enough to boil 4 bagels at a time.

6. Spread the ricotta mixture lengthwise down the middle of each rectangle, leaving a 1-inch border all around. Roll these up like you would a burrito, pinching and sealing the dough at the end. The trick here is to make sure you seal firmly by using your fingers to pinch the dough shut so the filling does not leak out. This will work only if there is no filling near the edge.

7. Drop the stuffed bagel into the boiling water and cook for 4 minutes.

8. Remove the bagels from the water with a slotted spoon and place on the prepared baking sheet, seam-

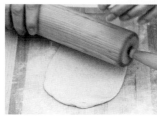

side down. Repeat with the remaining bagels, bringing the water back to a boil between batches.

9. Sprinkle each stuffed bagel with the sesame seeds. Make 3 small slits to release steam and bake until golden brown, about 20 minutes.

KIM'S HINT: You can make these cinnamon-apple style by replacing the vegan ricotta cheese filling with chopped apples, cinnamon, Sucanat, raisins, and walnuts.

THAI TOFU WRAPS

The tofu filling for these wraps is full of Thai flavors, with the perfect combination of peanuts, lime, and cilantro.

One 14-ounce block extra-firm tofu

¼ cup natural peanut butter (100 percent peanuts)

1 tablespoon low-sodium soy sauce

1½ tablespoons lime juice

¼ teaspoon garlic powder

2 teaspoons Sriracha

⅓ cup diced red bell pepper

¼ cup sliced green onion

¼ cup chopped fresh cilantro

6 whole wheat tortilla wraps

2 cups sprouts

Yields: 6 wraps
Prep Time: 15 minutes   *Cook Time:* 0 minutes

1. Drain the tofu and gently press between layers of paper towels to remove excess moisture.

2. In a bowl, combine the peanut butter, soy sauce, lime juice, garlic powder, and Sriracha.

3. Add the tofu, bell pepper, green onion, and cilantro. Stir with a fork until well mixed and the tofu is crumbly.

4. Place a portion of the tofu mixture in the center of a whole wheat tortilla wrap, top with sprouts or your favorite veggies, and roll up the tortilla. Repeat with the remaining tortillas.

> **KIM'S HINT:** You can also serve the Thai tofu filling in a sandwich. For example, try serving it on toasted whole wheat bread with fresh basil.

PATTY JONES, A woman in her late forties, owns and operates two daycare centers. She's energetic and outgoing. But she also had some serious health problems, including high cholesterol and type 2 diabetes. Patty was on two medications for her diabetes, but her condition wasn't improving. In fact, her doctor told her that she would soon need to take insulin as well. But then she heard a presentation at her church given by Nelson Campbell on the benefits of a plant-based diet. She immediately signed up for the 10-day Jumpstart program.

After five months on a plant-based diet, Patty had totally reversed her type 2 diabetes. Her doctor had given her a statin drug to lower her elevated cholesterol, but Patty trusted her plant-based diet instead, and her cholesterol went down 60 points. She said, "I never opened the bottle. I don't even know where the medicine is. I didn't tell [my doctor] that, but it was all because of the plant-based diet. People always say at the end of their rainbow, they plan to find gold. Well at the end of my rainbow, I found the plant-based diet. That was my cure."

ENTRÉES

BBQ Black Beans and Corn over Quinoa

A slightly sweet and smoky dish that feels traditional, this recipe is easy to prepare and goes perfectly with nutty quinoa.

1 cup quinoa

2 cups water

3 tablespoons Sucanat

2 teaspoons smoked paprika

⅓ cup low-sodium soy sauce

⅓ cup vegan Worcestershire sauce

3 garlic cloves, minced

½ cup low-sodium ketchup (no high-fructose corn syrup)

1 tablespoon dry mustard

1 tablespoon chili powder

1½ teaspoons liquid smoke

One 15-ounce can black beans, rinsed and drained

2 cups corn (fresh or frozen)

Yields: 4 servings
Prep Time: 15 minutes   *Cook Time:* 30 minutes

1. Rinse the quinoa, which can have a bitter taste if not rinsed thoroughly. Add the quinoa and the water to a pot, bring to a boil over medium-high heat, then reduce the heat to a simmer. Cover and cook until all the liquid is absorbed.

2. In a saucepan over medium heat, combine the Sucanat, paprika, soy sauce, Worcestershire sauce, garlic, ketchup, mustard, chili powder, and liquid smoke. Cook, stirring continuously, for 10–15 minutes. This will reduce and slightly thicken the sauce.

3. Add the beans and corn to the saucepan and allow to simmer for at least 15 minutes.

4. Serve over the quinoa.

KIM'S HINT: I like to add red bell peppers (my favorite vegetable) or a diced poblano pepper for extra spice.

BEANIE VEGGIE LOAF

The chickpeas and walnuts help the texture of this dish approximate real meatloaf. Try experimenting with other types of beans to find your perfect combination. This dish is rich in flavors and full of veggies and fiber.

½ cup low-sodium ketchup (no high-fructose corn syrup)

2 tablespoons molasses

1 tablespoon Dijon mustard

1 teaspoon chili powder

¾ cup water, divided

3 tablespoons flax meal

1 onion, diced

3 celery stalks, finely diced

3 garlic cloves, minced

1 green or red bell pepper, seeded and diced

¼ cup vegetable stock, for sautéing, plus more as needed

1½ cups canned chickpeas, rinsed and drained

1 cup dry oats

1 cup whole wheat bread crumbs

1 cup shredded carrot

¾ cup finely chopped walnuts

2 tablespoons chili powder

1 teaspoon dried oregano

2 tablespoons vegan Worcestershire sauce

½ teaspoon sea salt

¼ teaspoon black pepper

Yields: 6 servings
Prep Time: 15 minutes   *Cook Time:* 35 minutes

1. Preheat oven to 375°F. Line a loaf pan with parchment paper and set aside.

2. In a small bowl, whisk together the ketchup, molasses, Dijon, chili powder, and ¼ cup of the water. This will be your glaze for the top of the bean loaf. Set aside.

3. In another small bowl, combine the flax meal and remaining ½ cup water and let stand while you are preparing the remaining ingredients.

4. Over medium-high heat, sauté the onion, celery, garlic, and bell pepper in the vegetable stock until tender.

5. In a large bowl, smash the chickpeas. Add the sautéed vegetables, the flax mixture, and the remaining ingredients. Mix thoroughly. If you do not have the consistency of "meatloaf," add more vegetable stock slowly until the mixture is moist and holds together well.

6. Spoon the bean mixture into the prepared loaf pan and even out the mixture with your hands or a spatula.

7. Pour the glaze over the top of the loaf.

8. Bake for 30–35 minutes, or until the glaze is caramelized and the loaf is solid.

9. Let the loaf stand for 20 minutes before slicing.

KIM'S HINTS:
- This dish is especially delicious the next day.
- We make "bean loaf" sandwiches topped with lettuce, tomatoes, and onions.
- Using parchment paper to line baking pans not only frees your dish of added oils, but it also makes cleanup easier.

Black Bean Enchilada Bake

This is an easy casserole-style dish that works well if you are cooking for a large crowd. I often refer to this as "Mexican lasagna."

1 onion, diced

1 tablespoon minced garlic

1 jalapeño pepper, seeded and minced

1 cup diced fresh tomatoes

1½ cups frozen corn

One 15-ounce can black beans, rinsed and drained

2 tablespoons lime juice

½ teaspoon sea salt

¼ teaspoon black pepper

1 teaspoon chili powder

3 cups chopped fresh spinach

2 cups Mexican-style red salsa (mild or medium heat), divided

8–10 corn tortillas

½ cup Daiya Cheddar Style Shreds, divided (optional)

Yields: 6 servings
Prep Time: 15 minutes   *Cook Time:* 35 minutes

1. Preheat oven to 350°F.

2. In a skillet over medium-high heat, sauté the onion, garlic, and jalapeño in a small amount of water until tender. Stir in the fresh tomatoes, corn, black beans, lime juice, salt, pepper, and chili powder. Continue to sauté for 5–10 minutes more.

3. In another saucepan, blanch or steam the spinach in a small amount of water for a minute or two or until wilted and bright green. Drain and set aside.

4. Using a 9 × 13 inch casserole dish, spread about 1 cup of the salsa on the bottom of the pan (this will prevent sticking). On top of the salsa, line the pan with 4–5 corn tortillas—this will depend on the size of the tortillas. It's fine if there is some overlap.

5. Spoon the sautéed corn and bean mixture over the tortillas and spread evenly. Sprinkle with ¼ cup of the Daiya cheese (this is optional; I make mine without Daiya most of the time). Layer the wilted spinach on top of the vegetables.

6. Cover the filling with 4–5 more tortillas. Spread the remaining 1 cup of salsa on top of the corn tortillas and sprinkle with the remaining ¼ cup Daiya cheese.

7. Cover and bake for 20 minutes. Uncover and bake for an additional 15 minutes, until slightly browned and crisp around the edges.

8. Let stand for 15 minutes so the casserole sets.

BUDDHA BOWL.

This is a simple recipe, just quinoa tossed with veggies and chickpeas. The sauce can make or break a Buddha bowl, and this sauce is amazing!

1 cup quinoa

2 cups water

1 cup broccoli, cut into florets

1½ cups chopped dinosaur kale

3 green onions, sliced

½ carrot, shredded

1 avocado, pitted and diced

½ red bell pepper, seeded and diced

½ cup halved cherry tomatoes

1 cup canned chickpeas, rinsed and drained

½ cup Sweet Tahini Dressing (page 138)

Yields: 4 servings
Prep Time: 15 minutes   *Cook Time:* 20 minutes

1. Rinse the quinoa, which can have a bitter taste if not rinsed thoroughly. Add the quinoa and the water to a pot, bring to a boil over medium-high heat, then reduce the heat to a simmer. Cover and cook until all the liquid is absorbed.

2. Lightly steam the broccoli and kale in a small amount of water until the colors are bright green.

3. Add the green onions, carrot, avocado, bell pepper, tomatoes, and chickpeas to a large mixing bowl along with the steamed kale and broccoli. Toss to combine.

4. Assemble the Buddha bowl by placing warm cooked quinoa in a bowl and tossing with veggies and chickpeas. Drizzle the tahini dressing over the top and serve.

KIM'S HINT: A Buddha bowl is a versatile dish. So, if you like, change the veggies, add baked tofu, or use any grain you prefer.

Buffalo Beans and Greens

On our last trip to Nashville, Tennessee, we discovered a great vegan restaurant, The Wild Cow. I had their Buffalo Beans and Greens and it was amazing. That experience inspired this recipe. If you are heading to Nashville, check out their menu online.

One 14-ounce package tempeh or tofu, cubed

1 cup oil-free buffalo wing sauce, mixed with ¼ teaspoon liquid smoke, plus more for serving

2 bunches kale, sliced, with stems removed

Two 15-ounce cans pinto beans, drained and rinsed

4 cups cooked brown rice

1 cup Blue Cheez Dressing (page 125)

Yields: 4 servings
Prep Time: 15 minutes   *Cook Time:* 20 minutes

1. Preheat oven to 375°F. Line a baking sheet with parchment paper and set aside.

2. In a shallow dish, marinate the tempeh in the buffalo sauce mixture for 1 hour.

3. Remove the tempeh from the marinade and place on the prepared baking sheet. Bake for 10–15 minutes, until edges are browned and dry, turning the tempeh halfway through so it doesn't overcook on one side.

4. Steam the sliced kale in a small amount of water just until wilted. Drain, then add the pinto beans and toss with the kale until warmed through.

5. To assemble each serving, start with 1 cup of rice, then add the kale and beans, and top with the tempeh. Drizzle with the Blue Cheez Dressing. Add more buffalo sauce to the bowl if you like it spicy.

CARIBBEAN QUINOA BOWL

This recipe is easy to make for any meal. Black beans, salsa, and pineapple give it a sweet Mexican flavor.

½ cup quinoa

1 cup water

4 cups chopped kale

1 cup canned black beans, rinsed and drained

1 teaspoon ground cumin

1 teaspoon chili powder

¼ teaspoon sea salt

¾ cup salsa (medium heat)

½ cup diced pineapple (fresh, canned, or frozen)

¾ cup corn (fresh or frozen)

1 cup diced avocado

¼ cup sliced green onions

Yields: 4 servings
Prep Time: 15 minutes   *Cook Time:* 10 minutes

1. Rinse the quinoa, which can have a bitter taste if not rinsed thoroughly. Add the quinoa and the water to a pot, bring to a boil over medium-high heat, then reduce the heat to a simmer. Cover and cook until all the liquid is absorbed. Transfer to a large mixing bowl.

2. Lightly steam the kale until bright green. Add to the bowl with quinoa.

3. Add the beans, cumin, chili powder, salt, salsa, pineapple, and corn. Toss until the ingredients are well mixed.

4. Top with the avocado and green onions and serve immediately.

CHANA MASALA

This dish tends to be very oily and rich when ordered at a typical Indian restaurant. For this recipe, I have taken out the oil and used a bit of coconut milk. This dish is even better as leftovers because the flavors become more intense the longer it cooks or sits.

1 onion, diced

5 garlic cloves, minced

2 teaspoons minced fresh ginger

½ cup low-sodium vegetable stock, for sautéing

1 tablespoon curry powder

1 teaspoon ground cumin

⅛ teaspoon cayenne pepper

1 teaspoon paprika

2 teaspoons Garam Masala (page 146)

1 teaspoon sea salt

One 15-ounce can chickpeas, rinsed and drained

3 tablespoons tomato paste

¾ cup coconut milk

Two 14-ounce cans diced tomatoes

2 potatoes, diced small

1½ cups frozen peas

Naan Bread (page 67) or brown rice, for serving

Yields: 4 servings

Prep Time: 15 minutes   *Cook Time:* 30 minutes

1. In a skillet over medium heat, sauté the onion, garlic, and ginger in the vegetable stock until tender.

2. Add all the spices and continue to cook over low heat for 1 additional minute.

3. Add the chickpeas, tomato paste, coconut milk, diced tomatoes, potatoes, and peas. Cover and simmer until the potatoes are tender.

4. Serve with Naan bread.

COSTA RICAN BEANS AND RICE (GALLO PINTO)

This is a staple recipe for Costa Ricans. It's a very simple dish to make that goes well with a green salad or a side dish of roasted vegetables.

1 onion, diced

5 garlic cloves, minced

1 red bell pepper, seeded and diced

2 tablespoons grated fresh ginger

1 carrot, finely diced

1 celery stalk, finely diced

1 jalapeño pepper, seeded and minced

¼ cup water, for sautéing

3 tablespoons vegan Worcestershire sauce

1 teaspoon ground cumin

1 teaspoon ground coriander

½ teaspoon sea salt

¼ teaspoon black pepper

2 cups canned black beans, rinsed and drained

3 cups cooked brown rice

1 avocado, sliced

¼ cup chopped fresh cilantro

4 green onions, sliced

Yields: 4–6 servings
Prep Time: 15 minutes   *Cook Time:* 45 minutes

1. In a skillet over medium-high heat, sauté the onion, garlic, bell pepper, ginger, carrot, celery, and jalapeño in the water until tender.

2. Add the Worcestershire sauce and spices to the onion mixture and stir to combine.

3. Add the beans and rice, and stir completely, cooking over medium heat until warmed through.

4. Garnish with the avocado, cilantro, and green onions before serving.

KIM'S HINT: 1 cup of brown rice with 2½ cups of water should yield about 3 cups of cooked rice.

CRUNCHY CHICKPEA TACOS

These tacos have some of the seasonings used in a typical California fish taco—although I must admit that I have never had a real fish taco, only the vegan versions. This recipe uses a hint of lime with cabbage and, of course, chickpeas.

6 corn or flour tortillas

One 15-ounce can chickpeas, rinsed and drained

½ teaspoon ancho chili powder

3 cups shredded green cabbage

1 cup shredded carrot

½ cup thinly sliced red onion

½ cup seeded and small-diced poblano pepper

½ cup sliced green onion

¼ cup chopped fresh cilantro

¼ cup Tofu Cashew Mayonnaise (page 139)

2 tablespoons lime juice

¼ teaspoon sea salt

1 avocado, pitted and sliced

1 tablespoon Sriracha (optional)

Yields: 6 tacos
Prep Time: 15 minutes   *Cook Time:* 0 minutes

1. Preheat the oven to 375°F.

2. Shape the tortillas by placing them in a nonstick oven-safe bowl and baking them in the oven until crispy, 5–10 minutes.

3. In a large mixing bowl, smash the chickpeas with a fork and sprinkle with the chili powder. Add the cabbage, carrot, red onion, poblano pepper, green onion, cilantro, mayonnaise, and lime juice. Mix thoroughly, adding salt last.

4. Divide the salad mixture among the taco bowls and top with the sliced avocado. Add Sriracha if you like your tacos spicy.

KIM'S HINTS:
- I use nonstick metal bowls to shape my taco bowls.
- These tortilla bowls are perfect for taco salads as well.

CURRIED POTATOES

This dish has an Indian flair with its combination of potatoes, curry, coconut milk, and chickpeas. This is a great recipe for the slow cooker, so you can arrive home to the sweet aroma of curried potatoes!

4 potatoes, peeled and cubed

1 onion, diced

3 garlic cloves, minced

2 teaspoons ground cumin

¼ teaspoon cayenne pepper

1 tablespoon Thai Kitchen Red Curry Paste

4 teaspoons Garam Masala (page 146)

1 teaspoon grated fresh ginger

1 teaspoon sea salt

One 14-ounce can diced tomatoes

One 15-ounce can chickpeas, rinsed and drained

1½ cups frozen peas

⅔ cup lite coconut milk

Yields: 4 servings
Prep Time: 15 minutes   *Cook Time:* 30 minutes

1. Place the potatoes into a large pot and cover with water. Bring to a boil over high heat, then reduce the heat to medium-low, cover, and simmer until just tender, 10–15 minutes. Be careful not to overcook the potatoes and create a mushy texture.

2. Drain the potatoes and set aside.

3. Sauté the onion and garlic in a little water until tender, about 5 minutes. Season with the cumin, cayenne, curry paste, garam masala, ginger, and salt; cook for 2 minutes more.

4. Add the tomatoes, chickpeas, frozen peas, and cooked potatoes.

5. Pour in the coconut milk and bring to a simmer. Simmer for 5–10 minutes.

> **KIM'S HINT:** Thai Kitchen curry pastes can almost always be found in the Asian section of most grocery stores. This brand usually carries green and red curry pastes. I consider these ingredients pantry items.

FETTUCCINE ALFREDO WITH ROASTED VEGETABLES 🌱

This creamy white sauce is tossed in fettuccine noodles and topped with seasoned roasted vegetables. It's hard to believe it's dairy free!

1 pound dry fettuccine pasta (brown rice or whole wheat)

¾ cup raw cashews

1 cup hot water

1 cup nondairy milk

2 teaspoons lemon juice

4 garlic cloves

3 tablespoons nutritional yeast flakes

½ teaspoon sea salt

½ teaspoon black pepper

⅛ teaspoon ground nutmeg

2 teaspoons Dijon mustard

1 red bell pepper, seeded and sliced

1 red onion, sliced

1 pound asparagus, ends trimmed

10 cherry tomatoes, halved

2 teaspoons lemon-pepper seasoning

Yields: 4 servings
Prep Time: 25 minutes   *Cook Time:* 40–45 minutes

1. Preheat oven to 400°F. Line a baking sheet with parchment paper and set aside.

2. Cook the pasta according to the package directions.

3. Place the cashews, water, milk, lemon juice, garlic, nutritional yeast, salt, pepper, nutmeg, and Dijon into a Vitamix or other high-powered blender and blend for 1–2 minutes. The texture should be smooth and creamy.

4. Transfer to a saucepan and cook over medium heat for 5–10 minutes, stirring, until completely thickened.

5. Place the bell pepper, onion, asparagus, and cherry tomatoes on the prepared baking sheet, add the lemon-pepper seasoning, toss to coat, and roast in the oven for 20–25 minutes or until vegetables become tender.

6. Serve the pasta with the Alfredo sauce and top with the roasted vegetables.

KIM'S HINTS:
- If you do not have a Vitamix, I highly recommend you soak the cashews overnight and rinse them before blending. This will reduce the possible grittiness of your cashew cream sauce.
- I like to roast vegetables that are in season. I often use broccoli, zucchini, or mushrooms.
- Blend basil or spinach into the Alfredo sauce for a beautiful green sauce.

FIESTA LIME TACO BOWL

This whole-grain taco bowl is filled with black beans, red peppers, and onions seasoned with a Mexican-style lime sauce and topped with fresh avocados, salsa, and creamy vegan sour cream.

4 large whole wheat tortillas

¼ cup diced onion

1 tablespoon garlic, minced

1 cup seeded and diced medium red bell pepper

½ cup low-sodium vegetable stock, divided

One 15-ounce can black beans, rinsed and drained

⅛ teaspoon cayenne pepper

2 teaspoons ground cumin

½ teaspoon smoked paprika

¼ teaspoon chipotle chili powder

½ teaspoon sea salt

1 tablespoon lime juice

1 tablespoon chopped fresh cilantro

4 cups mixed salad greens

1 avocado, pitted, peeled, and sliced, divided

2 cups chunky tomato salsa, divided

¼ cup Vegan Sour Cream (page 144), divided

Yields: 4 servings
Prep Time: 15 minutes   *Cook Time:* 10–15 minutes

1. Preheat oven to 375°F.

2. Shape the tortillas into bowls by placing them in a nonstick tortilla bowl maker and baking them in the oven for 8–14 minutes until crispy but not dark brown.

3. In a large saucepan over medium-high heat, sauté the onion, garlic, and bell pepper in ¼ cup of the vegetable stock.

4. Add the black beans, cayenne, cumin, paprika, chili powder, salt, lime juice, and remaining ¼ cup of the vegetable stock. Turn the heat to medium and allow the mixture to heat through for 10–15 minutes. Stir continuously to prevent burning.

5. After the beans and vegetables have cooked down and thickened, remove from the heat and stir in the cilantro.

6. Fill each tortilla bowl with 1 cup of the mixed salad greens and ½ cup of the bean mixture, and then top with ¼ of the avocado slices, ½ cup salsa, and 1 tablespoon vegan sour cream.

KIM'S HINTS:
- I love using tortilla bowls to build salads.
- Tortilla bowls can be prepared a day or two ahead of time and stored in bags.
- You can make flour or corn tortilla bowls using any oven-safe bowl. Simply shape the tortilla inside the bowl, place in the oven, and bake until crispy.
- You can also skip the first step and, instead of making tortilla bowls, simply make burritos or wraps.

GARDEN PIZZA

The key to a great pizza is the dough. I love the artisanal pizza crust in this recipe. I also like to use a pizza stone because it cooks evenly with a perfect, crispy texture. I always make lots of extra pizza because we love having leftovers.

1 red bell pepper, seeded and sliced

1 red onion, sliced

6 ounces mushrooms, sliced

6 garlic cloves, chopped

¼ teaspoon sea salt

¼ teaspoon black pepper

12 ounces fresh spinach

1 recipe Artisanal Vegan Pizza Dough (page 59)

3 cups Marinara Sauce (page 136)

One 6-ounce can black olives (not packed in oil), sliced

¼ cup Vegan Parmesan Sprinkle (page 148)

1 teaspoon Italian Seasoning (page 147)

Yields: Two 14- to 15-inch pizzas
Prep Time: 30 minutes   *Cook Time:* 30 minutes

1. Preheat oven to 400°F. Line a baking sheet with parchment paper and set aside.

2. In a bowl, combine the bell pepper, onion, mushrooms, garlic, salt, and pepper. Toss well to coat with seasonings.

3. Spread the vegetables on the prepared baking sheet. Roast in the oven for 15 minutes, then remove and set aside, keeping the oven heated.

4. Wilt the spinach briefly in a frying pan using a small amount of water.

5. Roll out the pizza dough (this recipe makes 2 large crusts), poke fork holes in the dough, and bake on a pizza stone or round pizza pan for 5–10 minutes.

6. Remove the pizza crusts from the oven and spread half the marinara sauce on each. Top with the spinach, roasted veggies, sliced olives, vegan Parmesan, and Italian seasoning.

7. Return the pizzas to the oven for 15–20 minutes longer.

KIM'S HINTS:
- Remember, this recipe is for two large pizza crusts, so if you are only making one pizza you will need to cut the recipe in half.
- Add any variety of roasted vegetables you like. I like to use eggplant, kale, artichokes, sun-dried tomatoes, and broccoli, but it mostly depends on the vegetables I have on hand or what is in season.

IRISH POTATOES WITH CABBAGE

Hearty mashed potatoes with cabbage and leeks, this dish is a meal by itself!

6 medium potatoes, quartered

½ green cabbage, julienned

2 leeks, washed well and julienned

1 onion, diced

¾ cup low-sodium vegetable stock, for sautéing

½ cup nondairy milk

2 tablespoons garlic, minced

3 tablespoons nutritional yeast flakes

2 tablespoons chopped fresh chives

¼ teaspoon sea salt

¼ teaspoon black pepper

Yields: 4–6 servings
Prep Time: 20 minutes   *Cook Time:* 30 minutes

1. Place the potatoes into a large pot and cover with water. Bring to a boil over high heat, then reduce the heat to medium-low, cover, and simmer until just tender, 10–15 minutes. Be careful not to overcook the potatoes and create a mushy texture.

2. Sauté the cabbage, leeks, and onion in the vegetable stock until tender, then strain to remove moisture.

3. In a bowl, mash the potatoes with the milk, garlic, nutritional yeast, and chives.

4. Fold in the cabbage and leek mixture and season with salt and pepper.

ITALIAN EGGPLANT CASSEROLE 🌱

This hearty casserole is layered with breaded eggplant, tofu, and marinara. Serve with pasta and extra marinara sauce.

1 eggplant

3 cups whole wheat bread crumbs

2 teaspoons Italian Seasoning (page 147)

1 teaspoon garlic powder

½ teaspoon onion powder

6 tablespoons nutritional yeast flakes, divided

1 cup whole wheat flour

1 cup nondairy milk

One 14-ounce block extra-firm tofu

3 garlic cloves

¼ teaspoon sea salt

⅛ teaspoon ground nutmeg

4½ cups Marinara Sauce (page 136), plus more for serving

Yields: 6 servings
Prep Time: 30 minutes   *Cook Time:* 45 minutes

1. Preheat oven to 400°F. Line a baking sheet with parchment paper and set aside.

2. Peel and slice the eggplant into ½-inch-thick rounds.

3. In a bowl, combine the bread crumbs with the Italian seasoning, garlic powder, onion powder, and 3 tablespoons of the nutritional yeast.

4. Place the flour in a small bowl.

5. Pour the milk into another small bowl.

6. Dip each eggplant round into the flour bowl, then the milk bowl, and then coat with the bread crumb mixture.

7. Place the breaded eggplant rounds onto the prepared baking sheet and bake until golden brown, about 25 minutes.

8. While the eggplant is baking, place the tofu, garlic, salt, nutmeg, and remaining 3 tablespoons nutritional yeast in a food processor. Blend until smooth and creamy.

9. Coat the bottom of a 9 × 9 inch baking pan with the marinara sauce. Add a layer of breaded eggplant rounds, a layer of the tofu mixture, and a layer of the marinara sauce. Add another layer of eggplant, tofu mixture, then marinara sauce, and finally top with the remaining bread crumbs from the bowl.

10. Bake for 20 minutes, or until golden brown.

JAMBALAYA

A delicious taste of a traditionally Southern dish, this jambalaya has lots of flavor and depth to it.

¼ cup diced onion

¼ cup sliced celery

¼ cup diced green bell pepper

¼ cup diced yellow bell pepper

¼ cup diced red bell pepper

½ cup sliced frozen okra

1 cup low-sodium vegetable stock, divided

3 tablespoons tomato paste

3 garlic cloves, minced

½ cup chopped fire-roasted tomatoes

3 tablespoons chopped fresh parsley

1 teaspoon dried thyme

1 tablespoon liquid smoke

1 teaspoon smoked paprika

4 ounces tempeh, cubed and sautéed

1 teaspoon sea salt

1 teaspoon black pepper

4 cups cooked long-grain brown rice, for serving

Yields: 4 servings
Prep Time: 30 minutes   *Cook Time:* 70 minutes

1. In a large saucepan over medium-high heat, sauté the onion, celery, bell peppers, and okra in a ½ cup of the vegetable stock until the onion is translucent.

2. Add the tomato paste, garlic, and fire-roasted tomatoes. Heat through, stirring.

3. Add the parsley, thyme, and remaining ½ cup of the vegetable stock and bring to a simmer.

4. Add the liquid smoke, paprika, and tempeh. Season with salt and pepper. Cover and cook over low heat for 1 hour.

5. Serve over steamed brown rice.

> **KIM'S HINT:** I also like to use a slow cooker for this recipe since it requires an hour of low heat to bring out the full flavors.

MACARONI AND NO CHEESE

This is a great kid-friendly recipe. The cheese sauce is butternut squash and cashew–based, which gives it a slightly sweet flavor. I typically put peas in this dish but have also been known to add onion, spinach, or even a few mushrooms.

1 cup cooked and mashed
   butternut squash

¼ cup raw cashews

1½ cups nondairy milk

2 tablespoons cornstarch

¼ cup nutritional yeast flakes

2 tablespoons Dijon mustard

¾ teaspoon garlic powder

½ tablespoon lemon juice

½ teaspoon sea salt

¼ teaspoon black pepper

12 ounces macaroni noodles
   (brown rice or whole
   wheat)

1 cup peas

½ cup panko bread crumbs

Yields: 6 servings
Prep Time: 20 minutes   *Cook Time:* 40 minutes

1. Preheat oven to 350°F.

2. Place the cooked butternut squash, cashews, milk, cornstarch, nutritional yeast, Dijon, garlic powder, lemon juice, salt, and pepper in a Vitamix or other high-powered blender. Blend until smooth and creamy.

3. Transfer to a saucepan over medium heat and whisk until thickened. If you prefer it thinner, add water.

4. Cook the pasta noodles according to the package directions.

5. Combine the pasta noodles, sauce, and peas in a casserole dish, and sprinkle with the panko bread crumbs.

6. Bake, uncovered, for 20–30 minutes, or until golden brown and bubbly.

KIM'S HINTS:

- Using frozen butternut squash is a huge time-saver.
- It's a good idea to soak your cashews for a few hours and rinse if you do not have a high-powered blender such as a Vitamix. This will help give you creamier results.
- You can add other vegetables such as spinach or broccoli.
- Try adding Mexican Spice Blend (page 147) to the sauce and green chiles and red kidney beans to the macaroni—now you have a chili mac dish!

MUSHROOM STROGANOFF

This is a creamy mushroom sauce loaded with flavor. I have experimented with many different kinds of mushrooms in this dish and they all work well. Wild mushrooms are a family favorite!

½ cup dry white wine

1 onion, diced

5 garlic cloves, minced

1 pound fresh button mushrooms, sliced

1 tablespoon paprika

2 tablespoons low-sodium soy sauce

2 tablespoons Dijon mustard

1 tablespoon vegan Worcestershire sauce

2 tablespoons whole wheat flour

2 cups nondairy milk

½ cup chopped black olives (not packed in oil) (optional)

Sea salt to taste

Black pepper to taste

4 cups cooked brown rice or whole-grain pasta

Yields: 4 servings
Prep Time: 20 minutes *Cook Time:* 20–30 minutes

1. Cook the wine, onion, and garlic in a saucepan over medium heat until the onion is softened, about 3 minutes.

2. Add the mushrooms and continue cooking for 5–6 minutes, or until the mushrooms darken in color, soften, and release liquid.

3. Add the paprika, soy sauce, Dijon, and Worcestershire sauce, stirring well.

4. In a small bowl, whisk together the flour and milk until smooth. Add the flour and milk mixture to the mushrooms and turn the heat to low.

5. Simmer until the mixture begins to thicken, 5–8 minutes. Add the chopped black olives, if using, and season with salt and pepper to taste.

6. Serve the stroganoff over brown rice.

KIM'S HINT: I always add a can of black olives, minced, at the very end of cooking, which gives the entire dish a meaty texture.

ORANGE STIR-FRY

This dish may require more time and ingredients, but it is well worth it! I love the tangy orange flavor and the crunchy fresh vegetables.

1 cup julienned carrot

3 celery stalks, cut thinly on the bias

1 bok choy bunch, cut thinly on the bias

1 Spanish onion, thinly sliced

2 cups snow peas

1 tablespoon minced fresh ginger

6 garlic cloves

2 tablespoons low-sodium soy sauce

1 tablespoon Sriracha

1½ cups orange juice

3 tablespoons cornstarch

One 14-ounce block extra-firm tofu

½ cup low-sodium vegetable stock, for sautéing

3 cups baby spinach

4 cups cooked brown rice, for serving

2 tablespoons sesame seeds

Yields: 4 servings
Prep Time: 45 minutes   *Cook Time:* 30 minutes

1. Preheat oven to 375°F. Line a baking sheet with parchment paper and set aside.

2. Combine the carrot, celery, bok choy, onion, and snow peas in a large bowl and set aside.

3. Combine the ginger, garlic, soy sauce, Sriracha, orange juice, and cornstarch in a saucepan and bring to a simmer over medium-high heat. Cook for 15 minutes, or until thickened.

4. Cut the tofu into ½-inch cubes and toss in ½ cup of the thickened orange sauce.

5. Spread the tofu on the prepared baking sheet. Bake in the oven for 20 minutes, or until golden, flipping halfway through.

6. In a large frying pan or wok, add the vegetable stock. Quickly add the cut vegetables and cook until tender, 5–8 minutes.

7. Add the remaining orange sauce to the pan and stir to coat the vegetables.

8. Add the baked tofu and quickly stir-fry until everything is hot.

9. Add the spinach and cook until wilted.

10. Serve over brown rice and sprinkle with the sesame seeds.

Palak Paneer, Tofu Style

This creamy spinach dish is full of Indian flavors. I loved the roasted tofu, which is the paneer (cheese) substitute. The tofu is added to a creamy spinach sauce and served over brown rice or with naan.

One 14-ounce block extra-firm tofu, cut into ½-inch cubes

One 13-ounce can lite coconut milk

1 teaspoon sea salt, divided

1 large onion, diced

6 garlic cloves, minced

1 tablespoon finely grated ginger

1¼ cups water, divided

¼ teaspoon ground turmeric

1 teaspoon Garam Masala (page 146)

1 teaspoon curry powder

⅛ teaspoon ground cloves

1 teaspoon whole fennel seeds

1–2 jalapeño peppers, seeded and minced

One 14-ounce can diced tomatoes

1 pound chopped frozen spinach

4 cups cooked brown rice or Naan Bread (page 67), for serving

3 tablespoons chopped cilantro, for garnish

Yields: 4 servings
Prep Time: 25 minutes   *Cook Time:* 30 minutes

1. Preheat oven to 375°F. Line a baking sheet with parchment paper and set aside.

2. In a bowl, toss the cubed tofu in the coconut milk and ½ teaspoon sea salt and let marinate for 1 hour.

3. Strain the tofu from the coconut milk, reserving the coconut milk. Spread the tofu on the prepared baking sheet and bake for 20–25 minutes, tossing every 5–10 minutes.

4. Place the onion, garlic, and ginger in a food processor and grind into a paste. Transfer the paste to a medium-size pot with ¼ cup of the water and cook over medium heat for about 10 minutes, allowing the mixture to slightly caramelize.

5. Turn the heat down to low and add the turmeric, garam masala, curry powder, cloves, fennel seeds, and jalapeño (use 2 if you like it spicier). Simmer for 1–2 minutes. Add the tomatoes and stir to combine.

6. In a separate pan, steam the spinach over medium heat with the remaining 1 cup water until completely heated through.

7. Transfer the spinach to a food processor and puree until smooth. Transfer to the pot with the tomatoes and spices.

8. Allow this mixture to simmer over low heat while your tofu finishes baking. Add the remaining ½ teaspoon sea salt and stir.

9. When the tofu finishes baking, add it to the spinach mixture along with the reserved coconut milk from the tofu marinade.

10. Serve over rice, garnished with the cilantro.

PESTO PIZZA

This pizza is a great alternative to traditional red pizza. It has the fresh garden taste of basil, fresh tomatoes, and sweet red bell peppers. A family favorite!

2 cups basil

½ cup pine nuts (other nuts such as almonds or walnuts may be substituted)

1½ cups silken tofu

2 tablespoons lemon juice

½ teaspoon sea salt

2 tablespoons nutritional yeast flakes

⅛ teaspoon cayenne pepper

¼ teaspoon black pepper

1 large red onion, sliced

2 red bell peppers, seeded and sliced

1 recipe Artisanal Vegan Pizza Dough (page 59)

3–4 large fresh tomatoes, thinly sliced

One 6-ounce can black olives (not packed in oil), sliced

Yields: Two 14- to 15-inch pizzas
Prep Time: 30 minutes   *Cook Time:* 35–40 minutes

1. Preheat oven to 400°F. Line a baking sheet with parchment paper and set aside.

2. Place the basil, pine nuts, tofu, lemon juice, salt, nutritional yeast, cayenne, and black pepper in a Vitamix or other high-powered blender and blend until smooth and creamy.

3. Spread the red onion and bell peppers on the prepared baking sheet and roast in the oven until tender and slightly crisp, about 15 minutes. Remove vegetables from the oven and set aside, keeping the oven heated.

4. Roll out the pizza dough (this recipe makes 2 large-sized crusts), poke fork holes in the dough, and bake on a pizza stone or round pizza pan for 5–10 minutes.

5. Remove the pizza crusts from the oven. Spread half the pesto mixture over each pizza crust.

6. Using thinly sliced tomatoes, cover the pizzas thoroughly. Top the pizzas with the olives and roasted bell peppers and onions.

7. Return the pizzas to the oven and bake for 10–15 minutes longer.

KIM'S HINTS:
- When time is short, you can buy premade whole-grain pizza crusts. Just remember to check the nutrition label to make sure they are 100 percent whole grain and dairy free. Whenever you are buying processed (premade foods), always read the nutrition label.
- Remember, this recipe is for two large pizza crusts, so if you are only making one pizza you will need to cut the recipe in half.

Portobello Mushroom and Broccoli Stir-Fry

Portobello mushrooms give a meaty texture to this stir-fry. The hoisin sauce is a thick, spicy-sweet sauce made of soybeans. Serve over brown rice or quinoa.

½ cup water, divided

2 tablespoons low-sodium soy sauce

2 tablespoons hoisin sauce

2 teaspoons cornstarch

1 teaspoon agave nectar

6 ounces portobello mushrooms, sliced, with gills and stems removed

1 onion, thinly sliced

1 red bell pepper, seeded and sliced

6 ounces fresh broccoli florets

Yields: 4 servings

Prep Time: 15 minutes   *Cook Time:* 10 minutes

1. In a small bowl, combine ¼ cup of the water and the soy sauce, hoisin sauce, cornstarch, and agave; stir to combine. Set aside.

2. Place the mushrooms, onion, and bell pepper into a nonstick skillet and add a small amount of water to prevent sticking. Sauté for 3 minutes.

3. Add the broccoli and remaining ¼ cup water and cook for another 3–5 minutes, or until the vegetables are crisp-tender, stirring occasionally.

4. Add the sauce and stir for another 2–3 minutes, or until bubbly and thickened.

REUBEN CASSEROLE

I love a Reuben sandwich so much that I incorporated the flavors and ingredients into a vegan casserole-style meal. My daughter claims it tastes like a breakfast dish because of the hash browns. Whether you choose it for breakfast or dinner, it's a hit!

One 20-ounce package frozen hash browns (no added oil)

6 ounces mushrooms, sliced

1 red bell pepper, seeded and diced

3 tablespoons nutritional yeast flakes

½ teaspoon garlic powder

½ teaspoon onion powder

3 cups fresh spinach

1 cup Russian Dressing (page 137)

One 14-ounce can sauerkraut, drained

One 6-ounce package Lightlife Organic Smoky Tempeh Strips

¾ cup Daiya Cheddar Style Shreds (optional)

Yields: 4–6 servings
Prep Time: 30 minutes   *Cook Time:* 40 minutes

1. Preheat oven to 400°F. Line a 9 × 9 inch casserole dish with parchment paper and set aside.

2. Thaw the frozen hash browns.

3. In a skillet over medium-high heat, sauté the mushrooms and bell pepper in a small amount of water until tender. Add the nutritional yeast, garlic powder, and onion powder, stirring to combine. Add the spinach and cook until it wilts.

4. Press half of the hash browns into the bottom of the prepared pan.

5. Mix the Russian dressing with the sauerkraut and spread on top of the potatoes.

6. Spread the sautéed spinach, mushrooms, and peppers over the sauerkraut.

7. Cut the tempeh strips into small 1-inch pieces and sprinkle over the vegetables.

8. Top with the cheese, if using, and cover with the remaining hash browns.

9. Bake, uncovered, for 20–30 minutes or until potatoes are browned around the edges.

ROASTED VEGETABLES

This is an extremely simple yet wholesome meal to cook. When my kids were young and I was not able to make dinner, they would chip in and make this recipe for the family. This is one of their first "independently prepared meals." Potatoes are the center of the recipe, but the veggies can be changed depending on what's in season. Serve over brown rice or on top of a bed of spinach greens.

2 white potatoes, cut into
    1- to 2-inch chunks

2 sweet potatoes, cut into
    1- to 2-inch chunks

2 carrots, peeled and cut into
    1-inch chunks

1 onion, cut into wedges

1 zucchini, cut into 1-inch
    chunks

12 ounces mushrooms, sliced

2 red bell peppers, seeded
    and cut into 1-inch chunks

7 ounces extra-firm tofu,
    cubed

Marinade

¼ cup low-sodium soy sauce

2 tablespoons red wine
    vinegar

1 tablespoon maple syrup

1 teaspoon molasses

½ teaspoon dried thyme

½ teaspoon ground cinnamon

⅛ teaspoon ground cloves

½ teaspoon black pepper

2 teaspoons finely grated
    ginger

3 garlic cloves, minced

1 jalapeño pepper, seeded
    and minced

Yields: 4–6 servings
Prep Time: 20–25 minutes   *Cook Time:* 1 hour

1. Preheat oven to 375°F.

2. Place the cut vegetables and tofu into a 9 × 13 inch casserole pan.

3. For the marinade, whisk together the soy sauce, vinegar, maple syrup, molasses, dried seasonings, ginger, garlic, and jalapeño in a bowl.

4. Pour the marinade over the vegetables in the pan and toss thoroughly with your hands. Cover with tinfoil and bake until the potatoes are tender, about 40 minutes.

5. Uncover and bake for another 15 minutes, until slightly browned on top.

Sesame Noodle Lettuce Wraps

Crispy lettuce filled with Thai-flavored noodles, covered with sautéed carrots, peas, broccoli, and red pepper, and then garnished with sesame seeds—delicious!

2 tablespoons tahini

3 tablespoons lite coconut milk

1½ teaspoons Sriracha

¼ teaspoon red pepper flakes

½ teaspoon finely grated ginger

½ teaspoon sea salt

1 tablespoon low-sodium soy sauce

1 tablespoon agave nectar

1½ teaspoons lime juice

4 cups cooked whole wheat angel hair pasta

1 cup diced carrot

1 cup frozen peas

2 cups broccoli florets

1 cup seeded and diced red bell pepper

¼ cup low-sodium vegetable stock, for sautéing

8 whole leaves romaine lettuce

1½ teaspoons sesame seeds

Yields: 4 servings
Prep Time: 15 minutes   *Cook Time:* 20 minutes

1. In a small bowl, whisk together the tahini, coconut milk, Sriracha, red pepper flakes, ginger, salt, soy sauce, agave, and lime juice. Pour over the cooked pasta and toss to coat. Set aside.

2. In a large sauté pan over medium-high heat, add the carrot, peas, broccoli, bell pepper, and vegetable stock. Cook until the vegetables become tender and heated through. Place in a bowl and cool completely.

3. Once all the ingredients have cooled completely, start to build the lettuce wraps. In each leaf of lettuce, fill with ½ cup of the noodles. Top with ½ cup of the vegetables. Finish with a sprinkle of sesame seeds. Serve chilled.

SPICY BLACK BEANS OVER RICE

Hearty, delicious beans are heaped over rice. This recipe is simple to prepare and bursting with flavor.

1 onion, diced

4 garlic cloves, minced

1 red bell pepper, seeded and diced

1½ cups low-sodium vegetable stock

2 cups ½-inch cubed butternut squash

One 14-ounce can diced tomatoes

2 chipotle chiles in adobo sauce, finely chopped

½ teaspoon ground cumin

1 teaspoon dried sage

1 teaspoon dried marjoram

½ teaspoon sea salt

3 cups canned black beans, rinsed and drained

½ cup bulgur, uncooked

4 cups cooked brown rice

2 avocados, pitted and thinly sliced

3–4 tablespoons chopped fresh cilantro

Yields: 4–6 servings
Prep Time: 15 minutes   *Cook Time:* 40 minutes

1. In a skillet over medium-high heat, sauté the onion, garlic, and bell pepper in a small amount of water until tender. Add the vegetable stock and butternut squash and simmer over low to medium heat until the squash is tender.

2. Add the tomatoes, chiles, cumin, sage, marjoram, salt, beans, and bulgur. Simmer over low heat for 30 minutes.

3. Remove from the heat. Serve over brown rice and top with avocado slices and cilantro.

KIM'S HINT: I love to add all the ingredients (except for the rice and avocados) to a slow cooker and let it cook on low heat for 4–6 hours.

SPINACH AND BROCCOLI ENCHILADAS

Whole-grain tortillas are filled with a hearty mixture of spinach, broccoli, and a bit of tofu. These enchiladas have an interesting cheesy flavor, perfectly complemented with Southwestern seasonings. Top them with Vegan Sour Cream (page 144) and salsa!

10 ounces chopped frozen spinach

1 onion, diced

12 ounces broccoli, chopped

½ cup water

3 cups salsa (medium heat), divided

1 teaspoon garlic powder

1 teaspoon Mrs. Dash Southwest Chipotle Seasoning Blend or Mexican Spice Blend (page 147)

8 ounces extra-firm tofu, drained and crumbled

2 tablespoons nutritional yeast flakes

2 tablespoons tahini

4–6 large whole wheat tortillas

Yields: 4–6 enchiladas
Prep Time: 25 minutes   *Cook Time:* 30 minutes

1. Preheat oven to 350°F.

2. Thaw and drain the frozen spinach.

3. In a large skillet over medium heat, sauté the onion, spinach, and chopped broccoli in the water until tender. Add 1 cup of the salsa, garlic powder, and seasoning blend.

4. Remove from the heat; stir in the crumbled tofu, nutritional yeast, and tahini.

5. Coat a square baking dish with ½ cup of the salsa, which will prevent sticking.

6. Divide the spinach and broccoli mixture among the tortillas, and spoon it down the center of each.

7. Roll up the tortillas and place seam-side down in the salsa-lined baking dish.

8. Spoon the remaining 1½ cups salsa over the top of the tortillas.

9. Cover with tinfoil and bake for 25 minutes, or until heated through.

SPINACH LASAGNA

This is an easy recipe to prepare ahead of time. In contrast to traditional lasagna recipes, this one is light, filling, and full of delicious vegetables. This dish is easy and versatile!

4–6 garlic cloves, chopped

1 onion, diced

8 button mushrooms, sliced

¼ cup low-sodium vegetable stock, for sautéing

10 ounces fresh spinach

1 teaspoon Italian Seasoning (page 147)

6¼ cups Marinara Sauce (page 136)

12 lasagna noodles, uncooked (brown rice or whole wheat)

1 recipe Vegan Ricotta Cheese (page 99)

Yields: 6 servings

Prep Time: 20 minutes   *Cook Time:* 60–80 minutes

1. Preheat oven to 375°F.

2. In a small skillet over medium-high heat, sauté the garlic, onion, and mushrooms in the vegetable stock until tender. Add the spinach and cook just until the spinach is wilted. Stir in the Italian seasoning. Set aside.

3. In a 9 × 13 inch casserole dish, assemble your lasagna in this order: ½ cup marinara, 4 noodles, half of the ricotta, half of the spinach-mushroom mixture, 1¾ cup marinara, 4 noodles, remaining ricotta, remaining spinach-mushroom mixture, 1¾ cup marinara, 4 noodles, and marinara. (Lasagna noodles are layered uncooked.)

4. Bake for 60–80 minutes. Brown rice pasta will cook faster than whole wheat pasta.

5. Let stand for 20–30 minutes before serving

KIM'S HINTS:

- If I am in a hurry, my cheat version of marinara sauce is a fat-free, low-sodium jar of marinara sauce combined with a box of Pomi chopped tomatoes. I season it with Italian herbs and a little nutritional yeast flakes.
- I make this lasagna with uncooked lasagna noodles, which shortens the prep time. I have used many types of lasagna noodles, but our favorite is the brown rice version.
- Instead of mushrooms, I also often use zucchini and roasted red peppers in the vegetable filling.
- It is also fun to make the vegan ricotta a pesto style by blending fresh basil into the vegan ricotta.
- This dish is even better the next day because the flavors are more pronounced and the texture is firmer.

Stuffed Portobello Mushrooms

When I was growing up, fresh mushrooms were almost unheard of in our small-town grocery store. I never had a fresh mushroom until I was in high school! Now you can find them everywhere in many varieties. They are a fungus and a good source of nutrients. There are many claims that these little fungus treats are very medicinal as well. I love how they absorb flavor and add a meatier texture.

4 medium-size portobello mushrooms

2 teaspoons balsamic vinegar

1 onion, diced

3 garlic cloves, minced

¼ cup white wine

½ teaspoon dried rosemary

2 tablespoons chopped fresh parsley

4 cups chopped spinach

1½ cups canned cannellini beans, drained and rinsed

½ cup whole wheat bread crumbs, plus extra for sprinkling

2 tablespoons nutritional yeast flakes

½ teaspoon sea salt

½ teaspoon black pepper

Yields: 4–6 servings
Prep Time: 20 minutes   *Cook Time:* 20 minutes

1. Preheat oven to 375°F. Line a baking sheet with parchment paper and set aside.

2. Wash and remove the stem and gills of each mushroom. I like to chop the stems finely and add them to the sautéed onions later.

3. Brush the mushroom caps with balsamic vinegar and place the mushroom caps, gill-side up, on the prepared baking sheet. Bake in the oven for 10 minutes or until edges become tender.

4. In a large skillet over medium-high heat, cook the onion and garlic in the white wine for 5–10 minutes until slightly brown and fragrant. Add the rosemary and parsley and cook for another 1–2 minutes. Stir in the spinach. Remove from the heat as soon as the spinach begins to wilt.

5. In a large bowl, mix together the onion-spinach mixture, beans, bread crumbs, nutritional yeast, and the sea salt and pepper.

6. Stuff the mushrooms with the vegetable mixture. Sprinkle the tops with a little extra bread crumbs. Bake for another 10–15 minutes, until heated through. Serve hot.

> **KIM'S HINT:** This recipe could be adapted with button mushrooms as well.

SWEET MAYAN BURRITO

This burrito is filled with sweet potatoes, black beans, and chipotle seasoning, and smothered with salsa and our special sweet vegan sour cream.

4 cups peeled and cubed sweet potatoes

2 cups canned black beans, rinsed and drained

½ cup diced medium red onion

⅓ cup seeded and small-diced poblano pepper

1 cup frozen mango chunks, thawed and drained

½ teaspoon chipotle chili powder

½ teaspoon ground cumin

⅛ teaspoon red pepper flakes

¼ cup low-sodium soy sauce

4 whole wheat tortillas

3 cups Mexican-style red salsa (mild or medium), divided

½ cup Vegan Sour Cream (page 144)

Yields: 4 burritos
Prep Time: 15 minutes   *Cook Time:* 25–30 minutes

1. Preheat oven to 375°F.

2. Place the sweet potatoes in a large pot and cover with water. Bring to a boil over medium-high heat; boil the sweet potatoes for 5–10 minutes, then turn the heat down to medium. Cook until the sweet potatoes are tender.

3. Drain and mash the sweet potatoes, then reserve for later use.

4. In a large mixing bowl, combine the beans, onion, poblano pepper, mango, chili powder, cumin, red pepper flakes, and soy sauce. Mix until well blended. Do NOT smash the beans. Fold the sweet potatoes into the bean mixture until evenly combined.

5. Fill each tortilla with ½–1 cup of the sweet potato and bean filling, depending on how large your tortillas are. Fold in the sides of each tortilla and then roll into a burrito.

6. Coat a 9 × 9 inch baking pan with 1–2 cups of the salsa. Place each burrito, seam-side down, side by side in the baking pan.

7. Bake for 20–25 minutes. Remove from the oven and allow to cool for 5 minutes.

8. Serve with the remaining salsa and vegan sour cream.

THAI CURRIED VEGETABLES

This is an easy-to-prepare dish that is full of Thai flavors.

2 tablespoons Thai Kitchen Red Curry Paste

1 cup lite coconut milk

½ cup water, plus more as needed

1 onion, sliced

4 garlic cloves, minced

1 tablespoon minced fresh ginger

1 jalapeño pepper, seeded and minced

1 asparagus bunch, ends trimmed, cut into 2-inch pieces

8 ounces baby spinach

1 bok choy bunch, cut thinly on the bias

1 napa cabbage head, shredded

2 cups mung bean sprouts

Sea salt to taste

¼ cup chopped cilantro

4–6 cups cooked brown rice

Yields: 4–6 servings
Prep Time: 20 minutes   *Cook Time:* 10–12 minutes

1. Whisk together the curry paste, coconut milk, and water in a bowl. Set aside.

2. Sauté the onion, garlic, ginger, and jalapeño in a large skillet over medium-high heat for 1–2 minutes. Add water 1–2 tablespoons at a time to keep the vegetables from sticking.

3. Add the asparagus and cook for another 2 minutes.

4. Add the coconut–curry sauce to this mixture and gently cook for 1–2 minutes over high heat, stirring occasionally.

5. Add the spinach, bok choy, cabbage, and sprouts. Cook only until wilted.

6. Lightly season with sea salt and remove from the heat. Stir in the cilantro. Serve over a bed of brown rice.

KIM'S HINTS:

- I love the Thai Kitchen curries. I always have the green and red curry jars handy in my fridge or pantry.
- Using lite coconut milk makes the dish lighter; you can also reduce the amount of coconut milk and increase the water.

TWICE-BAKED BROCCOLI POTATOES

These baked potatoes are stuffed with seasoned creamy mashed potatoes and broccoli. They make a hearty dinner when paired with a side vegetable or a green salad. I love it for leftovers and it makes a perfect lunchbox meal!

4 medium-size russet potatoes

1 cup nondairy milk

¼ cup nutritional yeast flakes

1 teaspoon sea salt

¼ teaspoon black pepper

1 onion, diced

2 tablespoons roasted and smashed garlic

1½ cups frozen broccoli florets, thawed

¼ cup vegan bacon bits

½ cup Daiya Cheddar Style Shreds (optional)

Yields: 4–6 servings
Prep Time: 15 minutes   *Cook Time:* 1 hour 20 minutes

1. Preheat oven to 375°F. Line a baking sheet with parchment paper.

2. Place the potatoes on the prepared baking sheet and bake for 1 hour, or until tender in the center. Let the potatoes cool completely before cutting.

3. Slice each potato in half lengthwise. Carefully scoop out the pulp with a teaspoon, leaving about ¼ inch of the potato skin and pulp intact.

4. Mash the potato pulp in a bowl with a mixer. Add the milk, nutritional yeast, salt, and pepper. You may need to add more or less milk depending on your desired texture. Gently stir in the onion, garlic, and broccoli until well mixed.

5. Using a large spoon, place enough potato mixture into each potato skin so that it is a rounded, hearty filling.

6. Place the potatoes back on the baking sheet. Sprinkle the top of each potato with bacon bits and cheese, if using.

7. Bake for 15–20 minutes, or until the tops are crispy and slightly golden.

8. Cool for 5–7 minutes before serving.

KIM'S HINTS:
- You can use either fresh or frozen vegetables.
- Make these Mexican style by adding corn instead of broccoli, in addition to pinto beans and chipotle seasoning.

VEGGIE BALLS

These meatless veggie balls are perfect with Marinara Sauce (page 136) or spaghetti sauce on hot sub sandwiches. The Campbell mothers (Karen, LeAnne, Lisa, and Erin) all have their own special version. Grandmom probably wins for the most popular veggie balls!

½ cup bulgur wheat

1 cup water

1 onion, diced

1 celery stalk, finely diced

½ cup finely chopped walnuts

One 14-ounce block extra-firm tofu, drained

1 tablespoon tamari

1½ cups fresh whole wheat bread crumbs

3 garlic cloves, minced

1 teaspoon dried thyme

¼ cup vital wheat gluten (optional)

¼ teaspoon ground nutmeg

¼ teaspoon sea salt

¼ teaspoon black pepper

Yields: 6 servings
Prep Time: 20 minutes   *Cook Time:* 45 minutes

1. Preheat oven to 375°F. Line a baking sheet with parchment paper and set aside.

2. Place the bulgur in a medium saucepan. Add the water, cover, and bring to a boil over medium-high heat. Reduce the heat and simmer for 10–15 minutes, or until all the water has been absorbed.

3. Sauté the onion and celery in a small amount of water until tender.

4. Meanwhile, coarsely grind the walnuts in a food processor and place them in a medium-size bowl.

5. Place the tofu and tamari in a blender or food processor and blend until smooth and creamy. Use a rubber spatula to push the tofu down onto the blades to ensure it is well blended.

6. In a large bowl, combine the cooked bulgur, sautéed veggies, blended tofu, bread crumbs, ground walnuts, garlic, thyme, wheat gluten (if using), nutmeg, salt, and pepper.

7. Shape the mixture into balls (any size you prefer) and place on the prepared baking sheet.

8. Bake for 30 minutes, or until the veggie balls are browned.

KIM'S HINTS:

- If you are gluten sensitive, you can omit the wheat gluten, but the veggie balls will be more fragile.
- The veggie balls will keep in the refrigerator for about a week. They can also be frozen, but this will affect the texture slightly.

White Veggie Lasagna

Loaded with colorful vegetables, this creamy lasagna is guilt free because you can have the creamy texture without the fat. I personally don't add Daiya cheese to this recipe, so I made it optional. This dish takes a bit of time to prepare because of its different components, but it's well worth the effort. It gets better the next day, so make a bunch!

12 lasagna noodles (brown rice or whole wheat)

2 tablespoons minced garlic

1 onion, diced

½ cup low-sodium vegetable stock, for sautéing

3 cups chopped fresh spinach

1 cup shredded carrot

1 cup broccoli florets

1 cup chopped fresh tomatoes

1 red bell pepper, seeded and diced

One 14-ounce block extra-firm tofu, crumbled

2 tablespoons nutritional yeast flakes

2 tablespoons tahini

1 teaspoon sea salt

½ teaspoon black pepper

⅛ teaspoon ground nutmeg

1 recipe Cauliflower Alfredo Sauce (page 129)

¾ cup Daiya Mozzarella Style Shreds, divided (optional)

Yields: 6 servings
Prep Time: 40 minutes   *Cook Time:* 40 minutes

1. Preheat oven to 375°F.

2. Cook the lasagna noodles according to the package directions. This recipe won't work if you don't precook the lasagna noodles.

3. In a skillet over medium-high heat, sauté the garlic and onion in the vegetable stock until tender. Add the remaining vegetables and cook until tender. Add the crumbled tofu, nutritional yeast, and tahini. Season with salt, pepper, and nutmeg.

4. To assemble the lasagna, spread ½–1 cup of the cauliflower sauce on the bottom of a 9 × 9 × 3 inch glass baking dish. Layer the lasagna noodles on top, then ½–1 cup of the cauliflower sauce, half of the sautéed veggies, ¼ cup of the cheese, if using, ½–1 cup of the cauliflower sauce (I put sauce in each layer twice—once under the veggies and once on top). Repeat one more time, ending with a third layer of the lasagna noodles. Cover the top noodle layer with ½–1 cup of the cauliflower sauce and the remaining cheese, if using.

5. Cover with tinfoil and bake for 25 minutes, or until bubbling along the sides. Remove the cover and bake uncovered for another 10–20 minutes, or until golden brown on top.

6. Let cool to set before cutting and serving.

ZUCCHINI CAKES 🌱

Although made with zucchini, carrots, tofu, and onions, these cakes have a flavor of the sea and a nice baked texture. Serve them over a bed of lettuce and top with Tzatziki Sauce (page 141).

2 celery stalks, finely diced

1 onion, diced small

2 carrots, shredded

1 red bell pepper, seeded and diced

¼ cup chopped fresh parsley

¼ cup flax meal

½ cup warm water

2 small zucchini, shredded

One 14-ounce block extra-firm tofu, drained and crumbled

2 cups whole wheat bread crumbs

1 cup Tofu Cashew Mayonnaise (page 139)

2 nori seaweed sheets, finely chopped (kitchen shears work great)

1 tablespoon Old Bay Seasoning

2 teaspoons dry mustard

1 teaspoon sea salt

2 cups panko bread crumbs

Yields: 6 servings
Prep Time: 30 minutes   *Cook Time:* 40 minutes

1. Preheat oven to 375°F. Line a baking sheet with parchment paper and set aside.

2. In a skillet over medium-high heat, sauté the celery, onion, carrot, bell pepper, and parsley until soft but still firm.

3. Mix the flax meal and water in a small bowl. Let stand for 5 minutes.

4. In a large bowl, combine the sautéed vegetables, zucchini, tofu, whole wheat bread crumbs, mayonnaise, seaweed, Old Bay, mustard, salt, and flax and water mixture. Mix thoroughly.

5. Shape the mixture into ½-inch-thick cakes. Carefully dredge the cakes in the panko bread crumbs to coat. These patties are delicate and must be handled gently to avoid having them crumble.

6. Place the cakes on the prepared baking sheet and bake for 30 minutes or until golden. Serve warm.

TOMMY PRIVETTE, a retired Methodist minister in his early sixties, was first diagnosed with type 2 diabetes when he was twenty-three years old, meaning he'd been taking drugs to control it for more than *thirty-five years*. He also had several other health problems, including obesity, high cholesterol, and high blood pressure, for which he was taking no less than *seven* daily medications. Tommy was suffering terribly from the side effects of his meds. These included painful bloating and swelling.

Before the Jumpstart program, with his daily prescription medicines

After four and a half months of eating a plant-based diet, Tommy was totally pain free and completely off five of his seven medications. He'd also lost 40 pounds. Tommy was elated, saying, "I think one of the best things for me is that I finally feel like I have some control of my life, whereas before I was totally out of control with my diet and with my body. And it's very empowering to know that you have a say in it and that you can make good choices."

After the Jumpstart program

SIDE DISHES

CARROT RICE PILAF

Plain brown rice isn't always exciting if you eat it often, so I like to add flavor and color to my rice. This is a simple yet colorful addition to healthy whole grains.

1 small onion, chopped

1 cup coarsely grated carrot

2½ cups low-sodium vegetable stock, divided

1 cup brown rice, uncooked

½ teaspoon sea salt

½ teaspoon black pepper

½ cup chopped fresh parsley

½ cup sliced green onions

Yields: 4 servings

Prep Time: 10 minutes   *Cook Time:* 45 minutes

1. In a pan over medium-high heat, sauté the onion and carrot in ¼ cup of the vegetable stock until tender, about 5 minutes.

2. Stir in the rice and cook until the rice browns slightly.

3. Add the remaining 2¼ cups vegetable stock, salt, and pepper. Cover and simmer until the rice is tender, about 45 minutes.

4. Stir in the parsley and green onions just before serving.

CAULIFLOWER RISOTTO

Made with cauliflower "rice," this risotto is a light and healthy alternative to traditional rice risotto. This makes a great addition to any entrée.

1 cauliflower head, cut into florets

8 ounces mushrooms, chopped

1 leek, washed well and diced small

3 garlic cloves, minced

½ cup and 2 tablespoons low-sodium vegetable stock, divided

¼ cup white wine

⅓ cup pine nuts

3 tablespoons nutritional yeast flakes

1 tablespoon white miso paste

1 tablespoon lemon juice

1 teaspoon dried dill weed

¼ cup chopped fresh parsley

½ teaspoon sea salt

½ teaspoon black pepper

Yields: 4 servings
Prep Time: 20 minutes   *Cook Time:* 15 minutes

1. Cut the cauliflower into florets and pulse the florets in a food processor until it forms rice-sized pieces (12–14 pulses).

2. In a skillet over medium-high heat, cook the mushrooms, leek, and garlic in 2 tablespoons of the vegetable stock until tender; transfer to a bowl and set aside.

3. Add the cauliflower "rice" and wine to the skillet and cook for about 5 minutes, until the wine has evaporated.

4. Add the remaining ½ cup vegetable stock, reduce the heat to low, and cover, letting it cook for a few minutes. You want the cauliflower to be "al dente" with a little texture so it isn't just mush.

5. Meanwhile, pulse together the pine nuts, nutritional yeast, white miso, lemon juice, dill, and parsley until it forms a dry paste-like consistency.

6. Remove the cauliflower from the heat and stir in the nut mixture until well combined. Stir in the mushroom mixture, salt, and pepper until well combined. Serve warm.

Green Vegetable Medley with Mustard Sauce

This bright dish has the perfect balance of sweet and sour.

2 teaspoons Dijon mustard

2 teaspoons lemon juice

2 teaspoons agave nectar

2 tablespoons white wine vinegar

2 garlic cloves, minced

1 teaspoon dried tarragon

2 broccolini bunches, trimmed

10 asparagus spears, ends trimmed

6–8 ounces mushrooms, sliced

1 cup water

1 bunch kale, sliced, with stems removed

Yields: 4 servings
Prep Time: 15 minutes   *Cook Time:* 10 minutes

1. Whisk together the Dijon, lemon juice, agave, vinegar, garlic, and tarragon in a small bowl. Set aside.

2. In a large pot, steam the broccolini, asparagus, and mushrooms in the water, stirring frequently.

3. When the broccolini and asparagus are tender, 8–10 minutes, add the kale. Cook until the kale is wilted and bright green.

4. Place the vegetables in a serving dish and toss with the mustard sauce. Serve warm.

MASHED POTATOES

This is a simple and easy recipe, but you can make your mashed potatoes unique by trying different variations.

4 pounds potatoes, washed and quartered

1 onion, diced

4 garlic cloves, minced

¼ cup low-sodium vegetable stock, for sautéing

1 cup nondairy milk

¼ cup sliced green onion

3 tablespoons nutritional yeast flakes

3 tablespoons chopped fresh parsley

½ teaspoon sea salt

½ teaspoon black pepper

Yields: 4–6 servings
Prep Time: 15 minutes   *Cook Time:* 35 minutes

1. In a large soup or stockpot, cover the potatoes with water and bring to a boil over medium-high heat. Allow to simmer over medium-high heat until potatoes are cooked through, about 30 minutes. Drain, place in a large bowl, and allow to cool slightly.

2. In a separate pan, sauté the onion and garlic in the vegetable stock for 3–5 minutes, until the onion is soft. Remove from the heat.

3. Mash the potatoes with milk until the desired consistency is reached.

4. Add the onion and garlic, sliced green onions, and nutritional yeast, adding a bit more milk if needed.

5. Add the fresh parsley last and mix well. Season with salt and pepper.

KIM'S HINTS: Here are a few of the variations I use when making mashed potatoes:

- Parsnip-Horseradish Mashed Potatoes: Add 3 parsnips to the potatoes while boiling. When mashing the potatoes, add 3 tablespoons of prepared horseradish.
- Kale Mashed Potatoes: Add 10 ounces of sliced kale to the sautéed onion and garlic mixture and cook until the kale is wilted. Fold into the mashed potatoes.
- Carrot Mashed Potatoes: Add 1 pound of sliced carrots to the potatoes and cook together. Complete the recipe as originally instructed.

Roasted Asparagus with Sweet Potatoes and Chickpeas

This summer dish is a delicious combination of vegetables. I love to serve it over a bed of mixed greens and make it a dinner salad.

2 sweet potatoes, cut into 1- to 2-inch chunks

12 ounces asparagus, ends trimmed, cut into 1-inch pieces

1 onion, sliced

3 garlic cloves, minced

¼ teaspoon sea salt, plus more to taste

¼ teaspoon black pepper, plus more to taste

1 cup canned chickpeas, rinsed and drained

¼ cup Balsamic Vinaigrette Dressing (page 124)

Yields: 4 servings
Prep Time: 20 minutes   *Cook Time:* 35 minutes

1. Preheat oven to 425°F. Line 2 baking sheets with parchment paper.

2. Spread the potatoes on one of the prepared baking sheets and bake until tender, about 20 minutes.

3. While the potatoes are cooking, toss the asparagus and onion with the garlic, salt, and pepper in a bowl until well coated.

4. On a separate prepared baking sheet, spread the asparagus mixture evenly and bake until the asparagus is tender yet still crisp, about 15 minutes, stirring halfway through. Remove from the oven.

5. Place the potatoes, asparagus, and chickpeas into a large serving bowl. Pour the balsamic dressing over the mixture and stir gently to combine. Season with more salt and pepper to taste.

ROASTED BEETS AND GREENS

This is a very simple recipe, but few people think to put the whole plant together in one dish. My mother-in-law always served beets this way, and they have great texture and flavor. The cook time for beets is long, but if you plan ahead it's well worth it. Beets are a superfood!

1 bunch beets with their greens

1 onion, sliced

4 garlic cloves, minced

5 ounces baby spinach

1 tablespoon red wine vinegar

2 teaspoons maple syrup

½ teaspoon sea salt

¼ teaspoon black pepper

Yields: 4 servings
Prep Time: 20 minutes   *Cook Time:* 1 hour 30 minutes

1. Preheat oven to 350°F.

2. Wash the beets thoroughly, leaving the skins on and removing the greens. Rinse the greens, removing any large stems, and set aside.

3. Wrap each beet in tinfoil and place them on a baking sheet. Bake for 1 hour, or until tender. (I poke mine with a sharp knife to check for tenderness.) Remove from the oven and let sit until cool enough to handle.

4. Remove the skin from the beets and cut into 1-inch cubes. Set aside.

5. In a skillet over medium-high heat, sauté the onion and garlic in a small amount of water. Add beet greens and spinach and cook until wilted and tender.

6. Place the beet cubes and cooked greens in a serving bowl and toss well with the red wine vinegar, maple syrup, salt, and pepper. Serve warm.

KIM'S HINTS:

- Instead of baking, you also can boil the beets, leaving the skins on. When they are tender (check by poking a knife in them), remove the beets from the heat, drain, and soak in cold water. When they are cool, you can remove the skins easily and cut into cubes.
- While handling beets to remove the skins, you may want to wear gloves because the beets will stain your hands.

ROASTED BRUSSELS SPROUTS WITH POTATOES

My father grew Brussels sprouts in the garden and we cooked them in a variety of ways. They are considered part of the cabbage family and have a very strong smell and flavor. I believe Brussels sprouts are best when roasted with potatoes and seasoned properly to balance the strong flavor. This recipe gives Brussels sprouts that perfect balance.

1 pound small red potatoes

1 pound Brussels sprouts

1 red onion, sliced

8 garlic cloves, chopped

2 tablespoons minced fresh
    rosemary

1 tablespoon agave nectar

½ teaspoon sea salt, plus
    more to taste

¼ teaspoon black pepper,
    plus more to taste

¼ teaspoon red pepper flakes

Yields: 6 servings
Prep Time: 20 minutes   *Cook Time:* 35–40 minutes

1. Preheat oven to 400°F. Line a large baking sheet with parchment paper and set aside.

2. Rinse and scrub the potatoes. Cut into quarters and place in a large mixing bowl.

3. Cut off the stem on each Brussels sprout and remove the loose outer leaves. Slice the Brussels sprouts in half. Place in the bowl with the potatoes.

4. To the potatoes and Brussels sprouts, add the red onion slices, chopped garlic, rosemary, agave, salt, pepper, and red pepper flakes. Toss to combine and spread on the baking sheet.

5. Roast for 35–40 minutes, stirring halfway through the baking time. The potatoes will be golden and the Brussels sprouts will be lightly charred when ready.

6. Season with more salt and pepper to taste. Serve immediately.

SPICY OVEN-BAKED FRENCH FRIES

Homemade French fries are easy to make and so wholesome. Who doesn't love French fries? They are a perfect combination with sandwiches or wraps, and it's fun to add seasonings to make them interesting. This recipe is our family favorite.

4 large potatoes, sliced into thin wedges

1½ teaspoons chili powder

½ teaspoon sea salt

½ teaspoon black pepper

1 teaspoon dried oregano

1 teaspoon dry mustard

¼ teaspoon cayenne pepper

½ teaspoon onion powder

½ teaspoon smoked paprika

Yields: 4 servings

Prep Time: 10–15 minutes   *Cook Time:* 40 minutes

1. Preheat oven to 450°F. Line a baking sheet with parchment paper.

2. Add all the ingredients to a large resealable plastic bag and shake well to coat the potatoes evenly.

3. Spread onto the prepared baking sheet and bake for 30–40 minutes, tossing every 15 minutes, until golden and crispy.

The Problem of Food Deserts

THOUSANDS OF DISADVANTAGED communities across the country have little or no access to healthy, nutritious foods—especially produce. These areas have been referred to as "food deserts." Large chain supermarkets have abandoned or never entered these communities. Instead, the only food options residents have are small mini-marts that don't stock fresh produce, or fast-food restaurants. Additionally, many of the people who live in these places don't own cars and/or don't have the time or money to travel outside the community to shop at the larger supermarkets that do carry fresh produce. For these people, there's literally no option to acquire healthy foods.

A perfect example of a food desert is an inner-city community in Louisville, Kentucky, nicknamed "Smoketown." The *PlantPure Nation* film crew met with a group of people who live in Smoketown and discovered that there once was a thriving produce market in the area. Said one resident, "I remember when I was young, downtown was nothing but fresh foods. We would come, and it'd be crowded because you're getting fresh everything." And what happened to that thriving produce market? "It's a parking lot now."

But the demand for healthy foods and fresh produce remains strong in Smoketown. Shirley Mae, owner and head chef at a popular local restaurant, put it this way: "It would be great, absolutely wonderful, if we can get our local farmers back growing our vegetables again, and where we can have decent vegetables, and not have to pay an arm and leg for them. We could afford our vegetables, and they'd taste better. Oh, they just melt in your mouth."

The Smoketown neighborhood in Louisville, Kentucky

SOUPS AND STEWS

BAKED POTATO SOUP

This creamy soup is loaded with the flavors of a real baked potato and topped with vegan sour cream and veggie bacon bits. This soup is a hit with our family and friends.

4 cups peeled and cubed
   yellow potatoes

2 celery stalks, diced

1 onion, diced

1 tablespoon roasted and
   smashed garlic

¼ cup low-sodium vegetable
   stock, for sautéing

¾ teaspoon sea salt

¼ teaspoon black pepper

¼ cup whole wheat flour

2 tablespoons nutritional
   yeast flakes

2 cups nondairy milk

½ cup Vegan Sour Cream
   (page 144)

3 tablespoons vegan
   bacon bits

½ teaspoon red pepper flakes

Yields: 4 servings
Prep Time: 20 minutes   *Cook Time:* 30 minutes

1. Place the potatoes into a large pot and cover with water. Bring to a boil over high heat, then reduce the heat to medium-low, cover, and simmer until just tender, 10–15 minutes. Be careful not to overcook the potatoes and create a mushy texture. Rinse and cool. Set aside.

2. In a saucepot, sauté the celery, onion, and garlic in the vegetable stock until tender.

3. In a separate bowl, whisk together the salt, pepper, flour, nutritional yeast, and milk, making sure there are no lumps.

4. Whisk the milk mixture into the sautéed vegetables. Keep stirring to prevent sticking and cook for an additional 5 minutes, or until thickened.

5. When the milk broth has reached its desired thickness, fold in the potatoes and sour cream. You can add more milk if the consistency is too thick for your liking.

6. Ladle into bowls, sprinkle with the veggie bacon bits and red pepper flakes, and serve hot.

BURGUNDY STEW

Burgundy stew is an inexpensive French cuisine dish. Beef is braised in red wine and flavored with seasonings and vegetables. This plant-based version is complete with carrots, potatoes, and mushrooms. Serve with rice or pasta.

6 ounces mushrooms, sliced

3½ cups low-sodium vegetable stock, divided

¼ cup small-diced onion

⅓ cup small-diced carrot

½ cup small-diced sweet potato

⅓ cup small-diced tomato

¾ cup small-diced white potato

½ cup dry red wine

1 tablespoon garlic powder

2 tablespoons vegan Worcestershire sauce

1 bay leaf

½ teaspoon sea salt

¼ teaspoon black pepper

Yields: 4 servings
Prep Time: 15 minutes   *Cook Time:* 1 hour

1. In a saucepot, cook down the mushrooms in 2 cups of the vegetable stock until reduced by half and thickened, 10–12 minutes.

2. Add the onion, carrot, sweet potato, tomato, white potato, wine, and remaining 1½ cups vegetable stock. Cook until the potatoes are softened, 20–30 minutes.

3. Mix in the garlic powder, Worcestershire sauce, and bay leaf. Simmer on low for 15 minutes.

4. Season with salt and pepper, more or less to taste. Remove the bay leaf before serving.

KIM'S HINTS:
- This stew can be thickened or thinned by adjusting the amount of vegetable stock.
- I also like adding baked tofu in small strips for a heartier version.

CREAMY AFRICAN STEW

This hearty stew is rich with flavors, colors, and nutrients. The coconut, peanut, and curry give this dish an exotic flavor. It's easy to prepare and very inexpensive. Serve as a stew or over brown rice.

2 onions, sliced into half rings

1 carrot, diced

3 celery stalks, diced

2 teaspoons minced garlic

2 sweet potatoes, cut into ½-inch cubes

1 cup low-sodium vegetable stock

One 28-ounce can diced tomatoes

1 tablespoon curry powder

1 teaspoon sea salt

¼ teaspoon black pepper

⅓ cup all-natural peanut butter (100 percent peanuts)

1 cup lite coconut milk

One 15-ounce can chickpeas, rinsed and drained

2 cups chopped frozen spinach

Yields: 6 servings
Prep Time: 15 minutes   *Cook Time:* 40–45 minutes

1. Add all the ingredients to a pot and cook over high heat until bubbly, 10–15 minutes.

2. Turn down heat and simmer for 30 minutes, or until the sweet potatoes are tender.

KIM'S HINT: I like to throw everything into a slow cooker and allow it to cook on medium heat for 2–3 hours. Turn the heat to low until you are ready to serve. The flavors are perfect after they have cooked for the day.

CURRIED CARROT SOUP

This soup is light and creamy. I love the slight flavor of curry and the sweetness of the carrots blended with coconut milk.

1 onion, diced

4 cups low-sodium vegetable stock, divided

2 pounds carrots, sliced

1 tablespoon minced or finely grated fresh ginger

1 tablespoon curry powder

1 cup lite coconut milk

½ teaspoon sea salt

Yields: 6 servings

Prep Time: 10 minutes   *Cook Time:* 45 minutes

1. In a large saucepan over medium heat, sauté the onion in ¼ cup of the vegetable stock. Add the carrots, ginger, and remaining 3¾ cups vegetable stock and stir to combine.

2. Cover and bring to a boil over medium-high heat. Reduce the heat to medium-low and cook until the carrots are tender.

3. Remove from the heat and carefully transfer to a blender. You may have to do this in small batches. Use a pot holder to keep the lid down so the hot soup doesn't explode. Puree until smooth.

4. Return the carrot soup to the pot. Add the curry powder, coconut milk, and salt and cook over low heat for 5–10 minutes to bring the flavors together.

ETHIOPIAN STEW

This is an easy slow-cooked or one-pot dish. It is slightly spicy, sweet, and rich in flavors. This recipe uses berbere spice, which is a key ingredient in many Ethiopian dishes. It's a combination of more than ten individual spices. It can be difficult to locate, but you can make your own (page 146). I also have purchased berbere through Amazon.

1½ cups dried lentils

4 garlic cloves, minced

3 tablespoons tomato paste

1½ tablespoons Berbere Spice (page 146)

5 cups low-sodium vegetable stock

1 red onion, diced medium

2 cups diced butternut squash

½ teaspoon sea salt

½ tablespoon agave nectar

2 tablespoons pureed ginger

2 cups chopped frozen spinach

Yields: 4 servings
Prep Time: 15 minutes *Cook Time:* 45–60 minutes

1. Put all the ingredients in a pot and simmer until the lentils are tender, 45–60 minutes. Do not overcook because the lentils will turn to mush.

2. Add water if necessary to thin the stew. I sometimes like to add extra tomato paste for a richer flavor.

MINESTRONE SOUP

This is a thick Italian vegetable soup packed with vegetables, beans, and pasta. It's easy to alter by adding more beans, less pasta, and more veggies . . . and it comes out perfectly every time.

1 onion, diced

2 celery stalks, diced

2 carrots, diced

4¼ cups low-sodium vegetable stock, divided

1 zucchini, diced

One 15-ounce can cannellini beans, rinsed and drained

1 cup thinly sliced green cabbage

Two 15-ounce cans stewed tomatoes

1 tablespoon tomato paste

1 cup diced medium potato

2 cups chopped frozen spinach

4 garlic cloves, minced

2 teaspoons dried parsley

½ teaspoon dried oregano

1 bay leaf

¼ cup nutritional yeast flakes

1 teaspoon sea salt

½ teaspoon black pepper

1½ cups uncooked elbow macaroni (brown rice or whole wheat)

Yields: 6 servings
Prep Time: 30 minutes   *Cook Time:* 1 hour 30 minutes

1. In a large stockpot over medium-high heat, sauté the onion, celery, and carrots in ¼ cup of the vegetable stock until tender.

2. Add the zucchini, beans, cabbage, tomatoes, tomato paste, potato, spinach, remaining 4 cups vegetable stock, garlic, parsley, oregano, bay leaf, nutritional yeast, salt, and pepper to the pot. Bring to a boil, cover, and reduce the heat.

3. Simmer for approximately 1 hour. Add the pasta and simmer for 30 minutes more. Remove the bay leaf before serving.

NEW ENGLAND CHOWDER

This chowder has the flavor of traditional clam chowder. I use sushi nori sheets to get that sea flavor and mushrooms in place of clams. It's creamy and full of flavor, and the texture is perfect.

2 quarts and ½ cup low-sodium vegetable stock, divided

1 onion, diced

3 leeks, washed well and white and green parts cut small

3 celery stalks, diced

1 carrot, diced

⅛ teaspoon red pepper flakes

3 large Yukon gold potatoes, diced medium

¼ cup water

¼ cup whole wheat flour

2 cups Cashew Cream (page 128)

10 ounces button mushrooms, chopped

1 tablespoon lemon juice

2 sushi nori sheets, torn into small pieces (kitchen shears work great)

½ cup nutritional yeast flakes

½ teaspoon sea salt

½ teaspoon black pepper

2 tablespoons vegan bacon bits, for garnish

Yields: 6–8 servings
Prep Time: 20 minutes   *Cook Time:* 30 minutes

1. In a large soup pot over medium-high heat, add ½ cup of the vegetable stock and sauté the onion, leeks, celery, and carrot until tender. Add the red pepper flakes and cook briefly.

2. Add the remaining 2 quarts vegetable stock and the potatoes, bringing them to a boil. Turn down the heat to medium and cook the potatoes until tender.

3. In a separate bowl, combine the water and flour and whisk until smooth. Add to the soup mixture.

4. Add the Cashew Cream, mushrooms, lemon juice, nori pieces, nutritional yeast, salt, and pepper. Simmer until the flavors are well blended and the consistency is creamy, stirring frequently.

5. Garnish with vegan bacon bits.

KIM'S HINT: Most grocery stores carry sushi nori sheets in the Asian section. I tear the sheets into small pieces. This will add that sea flavor to your soup.

Split Pea Soup

This soup has a sweet, creamy texture with the perfect balance of spices. My children ate this soup often when they were babies and to this day love this soup with garlic bread or seasoned pasta.

6–8 cups low-sodium vegetable stock (begin with 6 cups)

2 cups dried green split peas, rinsed

1 onion, diced

1 potato, diced

2 carrots, diced

2 celery stalks, diced

4 garlic cloves, minced

½ teaspoon dried marjoram

½ teaspoon dried basil

¼ teaspoon ground cumin

1 bay leaf

1 teaspoon sea salt

½ teaspoon black pepper

Yields: 4–6 servings
Prep Time: 15 minutes   *Cook Time:* 2 hours

1. Place all the ingredients except the salt and pepper in a pot and bring to a boil over medium-high heat.

2. Reduce the heat and simmer until the split peas are tender, about 2 hours. You do not want split pea soup to have a crunchy texture, so be sure to give it plenty of time to cook. You may have to add more water or vegetable stock throughout the cooking if it gets too thick.

3. Add salt and pepper. Remove the bay leaf before serving.

Kim's Hints:

- When making this recipe, you will need to plan ahead because the dried split peas require a good deal of cook time.
- I have used my slow cooker for this recipe, and a pressure cooker works beautifully, too.
- Adding a couple of cups of chopped fresh or frozen baby spinach a few minutes before serving makes this soup even more delicious and nutritious.
- I sometimes use sweet potatoes instead of white potatoes.

SWEET PEPPER—COCONUT CORN CHOWDER

My niece, Kelly, went to Africa as a volunteer nurse. She quickly discovered that the local population did not have heart disease, diabetes, and cancer at the rates prevalent in our own country. It was during that time she decided to become a plant-based eater. She brought this recipe back and shared it with us, and it has been a family favorite ever since. Every time I cook this recipe, I think of Kelly's passion to practice preventive medicine. She is a nurse practitioner today in Pennsylvania. Thank you, sweet Kelly!

2 leeks, washed well and sliced

3 carrots, diced

3 garlic cloves, minced

1 jalapeño pepper, seeded and minced

2 red bell peppers, seeded and diced

1 cup water

2 cups frozen corn

One 14-ounce can lite coconut milk

3 tablespoons nutritional yeast flakes

¼ teaspoon black pepper

1 teaspoon sea salt

Two 14-ounce cans chickpeas, rinsed and drained

Yields: 6 servings
Prep Time: 20 minutes   *Cook Time:* 35 minutes

1. In a stockpot over medium-high heat, sauté the leeks, carrots, garlic, jalapeño pepper, and bell peppers in the water until tender.

2. Add the remaining ingredients and simmer for 10 minutes.

3. Scoop out one-third of the mixture and process in a blender until smooth. Add the mixture from the blender back to the pot and simmer for another 10 minutes.

KIM'S HINTS:
- If you prefer the chowder thinner, add more water.
- Serve this colorful dish with brown rice and a mixed green salad for a perfect meal.

WHITE BEAN CHILI

This is a nice alternative to red chili. It has a Southwestern flair and is chock-full of vegetables and beans. A true crowd-pleaser!

Two 15-ounce cans cannellini beans, rinsed and drained, divided

2 cups vegetable stock, divided

1 celery stalk, diced

1 onion, diced

4 garlic cloves, minced

1 jalapeño pepper, seeded and minced

1 red bell pepper, seeded and diced

2 tablespoons chopped fresh cilantro

1 cup frozen corn

1½ cups canned white hominy, rinsed and drained

½ teaspoon ground cumin

½ teaspoon ground coriander

1 teaspoon chili powder

2 tablespoons nutritional yeast flakes

2 teaspoons lime juice

One 8-ounce can green chili peppers

¾ teaspoon sea salt

¼ teaspoon black pepper

Yields: 4–6 servings
Prep Time: 20 minutes   *Cook Time:* 30 minutes

1. Place half of the cannellini beans in a blender with 1 cup of the vegetable stock and blend until smooth and creamy.

2. In a large soup pot over medium-high heat, sauté the celery, onion, garlic, jalapeño, and bell pepper in ½ cup of the vegetable stock.

3. To the pot of vegetables, add the remaining ½ cup vegetable stock, the remaining half of the beans, the creamy bean mixture, and the remaining ingredients. Cook over medium heat for 20–30 minutes or until vegetables are tender and broth is creamy.

TAKING BACK AGRICULTURE FROM AGRIBUSINESS

AN IMPORTANT POINT made in *Plant-Pure Nation* is the idea that plant-based nutrition could help regenerate the small family farm. Nothing used to be as all-American as the family farm. In 1935, their number peaked at 6.8 million. Today, less than a third—about two million—remain, and of these many are part-time or hobby farms. Much of the land that once belonged to small family farmers has been lost to development or to large agribusiness, now the dominant form of agriculture in America.

Because this type of farming is built on economies of scale—efficiencies improve with size—it's capital intensive, requiring large amounts of money to buy the land and equipment necessary to start and keep these operations running. One aspect of this is mono-cropping, where big corporate farms grow huge amounts of a single crop—such as corn—that is often used to feed the livestock that support our modern diet of animal-based foods as well as in the production of processed foods. Federal farm subsidy policies also have evolved to favor the large agribusiness operations and their crops at the expense of the small family farmer and a more diverse agricultural output.

With the wider adoption of a plant-based diet, *PlantPure Nation* argues, communities would start to reverse the ratio of their consumption of produce to animal-based products, increasing their total produce consumption from 5 to 10 percent to perhaps 50 percent or more. This much larger demand for produce would then create a viable business model for smaller, local farmers to supply this fresh produce to local markets. Because of their proximity to the market, small local farms can deliver fresher and healthier food more effectively than can the more distant agribusiness operations.

Comments from plant-based eaters indicate that when they start eating this way, they begin to think more seriously about where their food comes from. They want fruits and vegetables free of chemicals. And they want high-quality produce. They don't want green, juiceless tomatoes that turn red in transit from a distant location. And they don't want corporations manipulating the DNA of fruits and vegetables behind closed doors where no one can see what they are doing. This is why you see growth in farmers' markets, increased interest in organic and non-GMO foods, and the farm-to-table movement.

So imagine if people in a community increased their produce consumption by 5 to 10 times. Imagine the opportunities for small farmers, distributors, produce markets, and food processors. The free market would jump into action to create a system for small farmers to supply into. In this system, a small local farm could beat the corporate farm from afar. This may be the ultimate David-versus-Goliath story of our time.

DESSERTS AND SWEETS

CARROT CAKE

This traditional moist carrot cake has no added oils and plenty of healthy carrots, applesauce, walnuts, and raisins. Top it with fresh fruit or soy yogurt and now you have a delicious treat!

3 tablespoons flax meal

9 tablespoons (just over ½ cup) hot water

1 cup Sucanat

½ cup unsweetened applesauce

1 cup nondairy milk

1 teaspoon vanilla extract

2 cups finely processed or shredded carrots

2 cups whole wheat pastry flour

½ teaspoon sea salt

2 teaspoons baking powder

½ teaspoon baking soda

2 teaspoons Pumpkin Pie Spice (page 148)

½ cup finely chopped walnuts

½ cup raisins

Yields: 8 servings
Prep Time: 15 minutes   *Cook Time:* 25 minutes

1. Preheat oven to 350°F. Line a 9 × 12 inch pan with parchment paper and set aside.

2. In a small bowl, mix together the flax meal and water. Let stand for 1–2 minutes.

3. In a mixing bowl, combine the Sucanat, applesauce, milk, vanilla, carrots, and flax meal mixture.

4. In another bowl, combine the flour, salt, baking powder, baking soda, and pumpkin pie spice. Add to the applesauce mixture along with the walnuts and raisins. Gently mix until all the ingredients are wet. Do not overmix.

5. Pour the cake batter into the prepared pan, smoothing the top with the back of a spoon.

6. Bake for 20–25 minutes, or until a toothpick inserted into the center comes out clean.

> **KIM'S HINT:** I like this carrot cake by itself, but for guests I will often frost it with my Creamy Frosting (page 291).

CHOCOLATE-AVOCADO PUDDING

Avocado gives this rich pudding that creamy gel-like structure. I don't recommend you skimp on the dates and agave because they mask the flavor of the avocado and allow the chocolate to shine through. Most people never know they are eating avocado! Top with fresh fruit and unsweetened coconut.

2 Medjool dates, pitted

2 fresh avocados, pitted and peeled

½ cup unsweetened cocoa powder

¼ cup agave nectar

½ cup nondairy milk

2 teaspoons vanilla extract

Pinch of sea salt

Yields: 4 servings
Prep Time: 10 minutes   *Cook Time:* 0 minutes

1. Place the dates in a bowl with warm water to cover and let sit for 15 minutes to soften. Drain.

2. Place all the ingredients in a blender or food processor and blend until smooth.

3. Divide among 4 bowls and serve.

KIM'S HINT: The sea salt is added in this recipe because a small amount of salt helps the flavors "burst." You don't need much, just a pinch.

Chocolate Chip Cookies

These are a family favorite. I use a small amount of peanut butter (or any nut butter I have on hand) along with applesauce instead of butters or oils. These have more of a cake-like texture instead of the crisp traditional cookies. They never last long and many young people have requested them from our kitchen.

1 tablespoon flax meal

3 tablespoons warm water

¼ cup all-natural peanut butter (100 percent peanuts)

½ cup unsweetened applesauce

2 tablespoons nondairy milk

1 tablespoon vanilla extract

⅔ cup Sucanat

½ teaspoon baking soda

¼ teaspoon sea salt

1¾ cups whole wheat pastry flour

½ cup vegan chocolate chips or carob chips

Yields: 18–20 cookies
Prep Time: 10 minutes   *Cook Time:* 10–12 minutes

1. Preheat oven to 375°F. Line a baking sheet with parchment paper and set aside.

2. In a small bowl, mix the flax meal and water. Let stand until thickened.

3. In a large mixing bowl, mix the peanut butter, applesauce, milk, vanilla, and Sucanat. When the flax meal is thickened, add it to the wet ingredients.

4. In a separate bowl, combine the baking soda, salt, and flour. Add to the wet ingredients along with the chocolate chips. Stir until the flour is absorbed.

5. Drop the cookie dough onto the prepared baking sheet.

6. Bake for 10–12 minutes, or until dry to the touch.

Chocolate Power Bites

CHOCOLATE POWER BITES

These are no-bake cookies that I refer to as "bites" because I make them small. They are naturally sweet from the dates and loaded with chocolate and walnuts. They taste like you're eating a candy bar without all the butter, sugar, and artificial flavors.

1 cup walnuts

1 cup pitted Medjool dates

¼ cup unsweetened cocoa powder

1 teaspoon vanilla or coconut extract

¼ cup unsweetened coconut flakes, for garnish

Yields: 24 bites
Prep Time: 15 minutes   *Cook Time:* 0 minutes

1. Line a 9 × 9 inch pan with parchment paper.

2. Place the all ingredients except coconut flakes into a food processor and blend until a thick dough forms. You may need to add a small amount of water here if the consistency is too dry.

3. Press the chocolate mixture into the prepared pan.

4. Refrigerate for 1 hour.

5. Cut into 24 bites and serve. Garnish the tops of the bites with coconut flakes.

CREAMY FROSTING

This is a rich, "buttery" frosting that uses cashews and tofu as the base. Use sparingly and refrigerate.

7 ounces extra-firm tofu

½ cup raw cashews or cashew butter

¼ cup agave nectar

¼ cup water

½ teaspoon vanilla extract

⅛ teaspoon sea salt

Yields: 1¼ cups
Prep Time: 10 minutes   *Cook Time:* 0 minutes

1. Place all the ingredients into a Vitamix or other high-powered blender and blend until smooth and creamy.

2. Refrigerate for 1–2 hours so the frosting will thicken.

KIM'S HINTS:

- This can easily be made into a chocolate frosting by adding ¼ cup or so of unsweetened cocoa powder. How much depends on how dark and rich you want the chocolate flavor.
- If you do not have a high-powered blender, you may want to soak the cashews beforehand or use cashew butter instead of raw cashews.

DATE BARS

This is probably the most requested cookie/bar in my house—sweet dates cooked to perfection, sandwiched between a nutty oatmeal crumble. They are wholesome and rich in flavor. I like to prepare these during the holidays.

2 cups instant oatmeal

4 tablespoons agave nectar, divided

½ cup unsweetened applesauce

9 tablespoons water, divided

½ teaspoon ground cinnamon

½ teaspoon baking soda

¼ teaspoon sea salt

1 pound pitted Medjool dates, chopped

3 tablespoons chopped walnuts

1 tablespoon lemon juice

1 teaspoon almond extract

Yields: 12 bars
Prep Time: 10 minutes   *Cook Time:* 30 minutes

1. Preheat oven to 400°F. Line a 9 × 9 inch pan with parchment paper and set aside.

2. In a large bowl, mix the oatmeal, 3 tablespoons of the agave, applesauce, 4 tablespoons of the water, cinnamon, baking soda, and salt. This should have a thick consistency.

3. Firmly press half the oatmeal mixture into the prepared pan. Reserve the remaining oatmeal crumble for the top.

4. In a saucepan over low heat, combine the dates, walnuts, remaining 1 tablespoon agave, remaining 5 tablespoons water, lemon juice, and almond extract, stirring constantly until thickened, about 10 minutes.

5. Spread the thickened date mixture evenly over the oatmeal crumble mixture using a spatula. Top with the remaining oat mixture and press lightly.

6. Bake until golden brown, 25–30 minutes.

7. Cool thoroughly and cut into 12 bars.

KIM'S HINTS:
- Silicone pans will not stick and you won't need to use parchment paper. Amazon and kitchen supply stores sell silicone baking mats, bread pans, muffin molds, and casserole pans that are very inexpensive. I highly recommend them if you bake often.
- Before cutting into bars, I like to drizzle a light coating of powdered sugar and water over the top for a garnish. This is not necessary and adds extra sugar, so special occasions only!

Hot Fudge Sauce

DATE NUT CRUST

Made from dates and walnuts, this is the perfect pie crust for a raw or refrigerated pie. I love to use this recipe and fill the crust with my Chocolate-Avocado Pudding (page 287).

1 cup pitted Medjool dates
1½ cups walnut pieces
1 teaspoon vanilla extract
½ cup shredded unsweetened coconut
½ teaspoon ground cinnamon

Yields: 1 pie crust
Prep Time: 15 minutes   *Cook Time:* 0 minutes

1. Blend all the ingredients in a food processor at high speed until you have a sticky consistency.
2. Press the mixture into a pie pan and chill until ready to fill.

HOT FUDGE SAUCE

This guilt-free chocolate sauce goes nicely on plant-based ice cream or fruit. You can make it less sweet by cutting back on the agave.

½ cup unsweetened cocoa powder
2 tablespoons cornstarch
1½ cups nondairy milk, divided
5 tablespoons agave nectar
½ teaspoon vanilla extract
Pinch of sea salt

Yields: 4 servings
Prep Time: 5–10 minutes   *Cook Time:* 3 minutes

1. In a small saucepan over medium heat, whisk together the cocoa, cornstarch, and ½ cup of the milk until blended.
2. Add the remaining 1 cup milk and the agave to the saucepan and continue to whisk until thoroughly combined.
3. Cook the mixture over medium heat, whisking constantly, for 2–3 minutes, or until it forms a thick sauce.
4. Remove the saucepan from the heat and whisk in the vanilla and sea salt.
5. Serve warm over your favorite dessert.

No-Bake Chocolate Pumpkin Pie

This easy no-bake pie with the perfect amount of pumpkin pie spice will remind you of the holidays.

1 cup vegan semisweet chocolate chips

¼ cup unsweetened cocoa powder

One 15-ounce can pumpkin puree

¼ cup maple syrup

¼ teaspoon ground cinnamon

⅛ teaspoon ground nutmeg

⅛ teaspoon ground cloves

¼ teaspoon sea salt

1 Date Nut Crust (page 295)

Fruit, nuts, or chocolate shavings, for garnish

Yields: 8 servings
Prep Time: 30 minutes   *Cook Time:* 0 minutes

1. Melt the chocolate chips either in a double boiler on the stove or in a microwave-safe bowl in the microwave.

2. Place the melted chocolate, cocoa, pumpkin puree, maple syrup, cinnamon, nutmeg, cloves, and salt into a food processor and blend until smooth.

3. Pour into the date nut crust and refrigerate for at least 4 hours. This pie gets firmer the longer it sits.

4. Garnish the top with fruit, nuts, or chocolate shavings.

NUT BUTTER BROWNIES

These are extra-moist brownies that are whole grain and have no added oil. The nut butter and applesauce give it a fudge-like texture for an extra-special chocolate treat.

2 tablespoons flax meal

6 tablespoons warm water

½ cup Sucanat

½ cup agave nectar

1 teaspoon vanilla extract

¼ cup nut butter

½ cup unsweetened applesauce

¾ cup whole wheat pastry flour

⅓ cup unsweetened cocoa powder

½ teaspoon baking powder

¼ teaspoon sea salt

½ cup vegan semisweet chocolate chips

Yields: 12 brownies
Prep Time: 15 minutes   *Cook Time:* 30 minutes

1. Preheat oven to 350°F. Line a 9 × 9 inch pan with parchment paper and set aside.

2. In a small bowl, mix together the flax meal and water. Let stand for 2 minutes.

3. In a separate bowl, blend the Sucanat, agave, vanilla, nut butter, applesauce, and flax meal mixture until smooth.

4. In a third bowl, combine the flour, baking cocoa, baking powder, and salt. Add to the Sucanat mixture and stir to combine.

5. Fold in the vegan chocolate chips.

6. Spoon the batter into the prepared pan.

7. Bake for 30–35 minutes, or until a toothpick inserted into the center comes out clean.

8. Let cool on a wire rack before slicing.

PINEAPPLE SORBET

If you have ever tried Pineapple Whip at Disneyland or the Dole Plantation in Hawaii, then you will be familiar with this recipe. This sorbet is a plant-based, healthy version that is creamy, refreshing, and satisfying. It's my new favorite dessert.

1 ripe pineapple
½ cup nondairy milk
1 tablespoon agave nectar
¼ cup lite coconut milk

Yields: 4 servings
Prep Time: 5 minutes   *Cook Time:* 0 minutes

1. Peel and cut up the pineapple, making sure to take out all the core. Freeze overnight. If you don't have time, you can use store-bought frozen pineapple.

2. Place all ingredients in a high-powered blender (a Vitamix works best). Blend until creamy. If needed, add more milk to get your blades spinning smoothly.

3. Divide among 4 bowls and serve immediately.

STRAWBERRY-RHUBARB CRISP

Rhubarb is a springtime vegetable that my dad grew in our garden. You cut and cook only the stalks, which are reddish to light green in color. Rhubarb stalks are very sour and cannot be eaten without cooking them down and adding a sweetener. Strawberries and rhubarb both come into season at the same time, making them the perfect dessert pair!

3 cups diced rhubarb

1 pound strawberries, hulled and sliced

⅓ cup and ¼ cup Sucanat, divided

½ cup and 2 tablespoons whole wheat pastry flour, divided

¼ cup pitted and chopped Medjool dates

½ cup whole-grain rolled oats

½ cup finely chopped walnuts

3 tablespoons apple or orange juice

Yields: 6 servings

Prep Time: 20 minutes   *Cook Time:* 40 minutes

1. Preheat oven to 375°F. Line a 9 × 9 inch baking pan with parchment paper and set aside.

2. In a large bowl, mix together the rhubarb, strawberries, ⅓ cup of the Sucanat, 2 tablespoons of the flour, and the dates.

3. In a separate bowl, mix together the rolled oats, remaining ½ cup flour, remaining ¼ cup Sucanat, walnuts, and apple juice.

4. Evenly spread the strawberry-rhubarb mixture into the prepared pan. Top with the oats mixture, spreading evenly.

5. Bake for 35–40 minutes, until golden brown and bubbly. Spoon into bowls and serve warm.

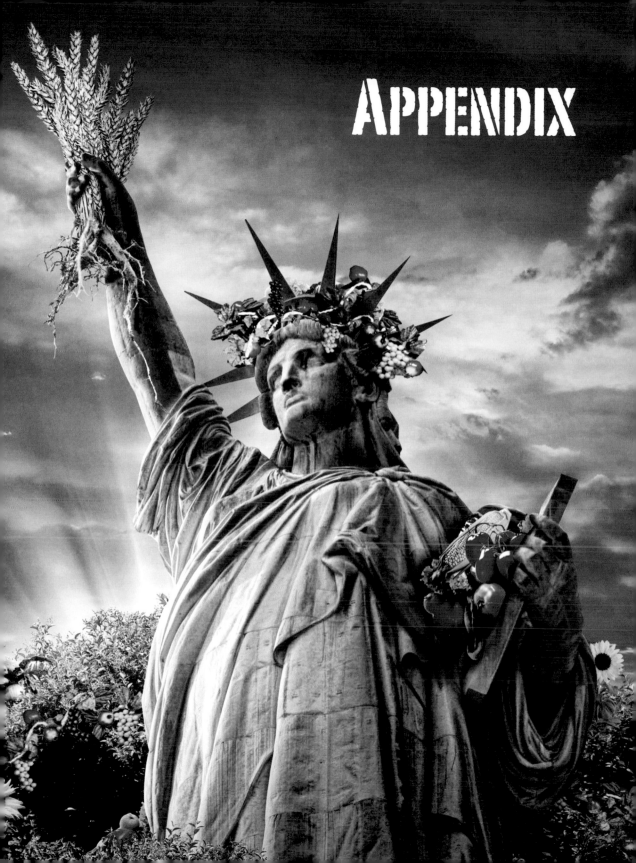

APPENDIX

DRIED BEANS AND LEGUMES COOKING CHART

Beans (1 cup dry)	Cups Water	Cook Time	Cups Yield
Black	4	90 minutes	2¼
Black-eyed peas	4	90 minutes	2
Chickpeas	4	120 minutes	2
Lentils	3	45 minutes	2
Navy	4	90 minutes	2¾
Pinto	4	90–120 minutes	2½
Red kidney	4	90–120 minutes	2¼
Split peas	6	90 minutes	2

Cooking dried beans is not difficult, just time-consuming. It can take anywhere from 1 hour to 3 hours (and sometimes longer) for them to become tender. Cook time depends on the type of bean and the amount of time you soak them.

Directions for Cooking Dried Beans

1. Wash and discard beans that are shriveled and discolored. Remove any rocks or debris.

2. Soak the beans. This helps cut down your cook time and allows the beans to cook more evenly. I recommend soaking them overnight (10–14 hours). Cover the beans with a few inches of water and leave them on the counter.

3. After soaking, the beans will double in size and absorb most of the water. Drain and gently rinse them in water.

4. Cover the rinsed beans with an inch of water in a saucepan and bring to a boil.

5. Simmer the beans gently for the indicated cook time.

6. Because salt can prevent the starches in the beans from breaking down, add salt in the last hour of cooking.

Grains Cooking Chart

Grains (1 cup dry)	Cups Water	Cook Time	Cups Yield
Barley, pearled	3	50–60 minutes	4
Bulgur	2	15 minutes	3
Cornmeal (coarse)	4–4½	20–25 minutes	2½
Couscous, whole wheat	1	5 minutes	2
Farro, pearled	3	45–55 minutes	4
Oats, rolled	1½	8–10 minutes	1½
Oats, steel cut	2½	30 minutes	2½
Quinoa	2	15–20 minutes	4
Rice, brown, long grain	2½	45–55 minutes	3
Rice, brown, short grain	2½	45–55 minutes	3
Rice, brown, quick	1¼	10 minutes	2
Rice, wild	3	50–60 minutes	4

Directions for Cooking Grains

1. Put grain and water into a saucepan, cover, and bring to a boil over high heat. Turn the heat down to low and steam for the recommended cook time. Lift the lid and test the grains for tenderness. If the grain needs more time, cover the saucepan and steam for 5–10 minutes longer. If the grain needs more cook time and all the water has been absorbed, add up to ¼ cup of water, cover, and continue steaming.

2. Once tender, turn off the heat and allow the grains to rest and fluff for 5–10 minutes before serving.

RECIPE INDEX

ACKNOWLEDGMENTS

This book would not be possible if it weren't for my family. They have been pushing me to put my recipes on paper and share everything I know from the years spent in our own kitchen. My loving husband, Nelson, is my biggest coach and fan. He has enough energy and enthusiasm for almost any task! Making the documentary was his final push for encouraging me to write this book. He is always trying to create opportunities for me to share my food knowledge with the public. Thank you, Nelson, for pushing me and always believing in me.

Thanks to our children, Whitney, Colin, and Laura, for teaching me how to be better! You three kids, along with the many friends you brought to our house, were always requesting, critiquing, and challenging me to cater to your taste buds. You always told me the truth! But, most of all, you three always light up my kitchen. Many of our greatest discussions happened at my kitchen island over numerous chopped vegetables.

Thanks to my mother- and father-in-law, Karen and Colin, for teaching me everything I know about the plant-based diet. I watched Karen cook plant-based for more than twenty-five years. She's a pro! She can cook for the entire family (and we are a large crowd), keeping the food healthy and delicious. And Colin's research and science made this book possible. He has taught us all so much about health, science, and the ways of the world. He is a brilliant man, but most of all, he's a loving and kind father-in-law.

Thanks to Karen Whiston and her daughter, Kelly Schillinger, for testing so many of these recipes and giving honest feedback. I have flooded your inboxes and voicemail with absolutely too much food information. Also, thank you, Karen, for teaching me how to cook when I was only seven years old; you are the root of my culinary passion.

I also would like to thank my mother, Mary Anne Pearce, for teaching me so many cooking techniques and having high expectations. You gave me the freedom to cook for our family at a very young age, always expressing gratefulness for my skills and the meals I prepared. Mealtime was family time and our dinner table was full of so much love and laughter. Thank you to my father, Carl Pearce, for planting huge gardens and encouraging us to love vegetables and prepare them well. How many rows of Swiss chard did you really plant? The strawberry rhubarb recipe is for you, Dad. The bags of vegetables you placed in the kitchen for us to prepare were truly a gift to our health, even if it looked like mundane chores to a twelve-year-old. I love you both for raising me to follow my dreams and teaching me to always put my family first.

Thank you, Kevin Dunn and Amber Gilbert, for your recipe contributions in this cookbook. You were both instrumental in giving birth to several recipes we used during our Jumpstarts. Your hard work and creativity made many of our Jumpstart recipes economical, easy to prepare, and delicious.

Thank you to Brian Olson, our photographer. It was a pleasure working with someone so talented and motivated. You have the artistic ability to make food look like a work of art! I also appreciate the feedback and positive remarks you made after every dish I passed your way. I'm looking forward to our next food project!

Our film crew, including John Corry, Lee Fulkerson, Frank Smith, and Brian Olson, has been fantastic. The hard work and long trips to Kentucky and other places were inspiring and fun. This crew managed to put a smile on our faces even when the going got tough. Thank you for all your efforts in this project.

About the Author

Kim Campbell is the daughter-in-law of Dr. T. Colin Campbell, considered by many as the "science father" of the rapidly growing plant-based nutrition movement. She works with her husband, Nelson, in a health and wellness business promoting a whole food, plant-based diet. This experience has allowed her to hone her culinary skills, especially in understanding how to create flavors, textures, and presentations that appeal to mainstream consumers experiencing a plant-based diet for the first time. Kim holds a bachelor's degree from Cornell University in human service studies, with a minor in nutrition and child development.

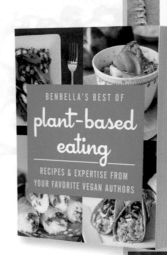